THE ART OF CHINESE KUNG FU

GINGKO PRESS

CONTENTS

TAO OF KUNG FU

A group of young artists with a flaming passion for kung fu and a keen interest to explore its mysteries are roving China. They are crossing bamboo groves, stepping into temples and monasteries, visiting martial artists, and shuffling between skyscrapers in metropolises. Whenever they look into the distance from the mountaintop, or watch bamboo stalks waving in the breeze, excitement surges in them, as unappeased as the ripples of wind through the bamboo grove.

Meanwhile, I have come to the Wushu Town, Qingzhen City, in Guizhou Province on the occasion of the Seventh National Wushu Championship. Standing on the lakeside lined with maple trees and facing the still water, I am lost in deep thought: What is Chinese kung fu? How is traditional Chinese kung fu going to embrace the modern future?

At twelve, I found myself in the traditional martial arts community by chance and thus started to practice kung fu in Jingshan Park, the so-called backyard garden of the imperial family. Half a century has passed, and I'm already in my sixties. In retrospect, I have found that only kung fu has benefited me all my life. If you ask for my own understanding of kung fu, I think I will resort to the Zen meditators' motto in answer: "A beginner will see mountain as mountain, water as water; when he starts to dive into Zen, he will see mountain as something other than mountain, water as something other than water; when he fully understands Zen, he will again see mountain as mountain, water as water." I have practiced kung fu for decades, and it always dawns on me that what I believed in yesterday is under fierce challenge today. I had my first access to traditional kung fu culture when I was still a boy. Thirty years ago, I embarked on a journey to rejuvenate the nation by seeking answers from Western technologies. Two years ago, I formally retired, and returned to the traditional martial arts. Today, I have founded the Martial and Medical Institute, which is focused on popularizing martial arts thoughts and medical ethics. If the martial arts community is compared to *jianghu* (literally translated as "river and lake"), I have been only walking along the lakeside.

In my eyes, kung fu has been incorporated into sports, dance, opera, lyre-playing, chess, calligraphy, and painting to different extents. Kung fu has not only infused artistic value into these traditional Chinese art forms, but also given them a unique cultural and spiritual association. Modern movies and comics, in particular, have transformed into new arenas for kung fu.

In China, kung fu has already evolved into an integral and omnipresent part of people's lives. The martial arts community used to say that martial arts and medical science are always developing hand in hand. Kung fu not only enhances physical strength but also helps maintain health. Martial doctors could enable people to explore the mysteries of life and the universe through constant comprehension of themselves.

Chinese kung fu is defined as miraculous and fierce, partly due to the influence of kung fu movies. In the modern era, kung fu has been overshadowed by some lethal weapons, but its identity as a combating technique remains unchanged. Unlike Western forms of combat, fierceness and force are not the only pursuits of Chinese kung fu. Instead, kung fu prioritizes the utilization of techniques and skills and application of force, all of which are based on a solid foundation. The most outstanding martial artist can always overcome a stronger rival by making strategic use of skills and force. Besides, kung fu is about a more profound pursuit: that is, to triumph over oneself.

In essence, Chinese kung fu is more about harmony and peace than combat. Kung fu practice involves physical training and enhancing spiritual edification. The practitioners are supposed to strike an optimal harmony between the physical, spiritual, and psychological senses. Chinese kung fu has three highlights: vitality, energy, and spirit. None of these three can be achieved without long-term enhancement of both internal and external elements.

Martial arts are not only about improving physical strength or defending against enemies, but also about demonstrating the inner rhythm with physical expressions. Therefore, martial arts are also an art form in essence. Through intensive training, a martial artist can achieve a harmony between his inner rhythm, nature, and life and so will come to understand the profundity of nature and the indefiniteness of life. If so, the practitioner has elevated himself to a new level that testifies to the Taoist philosophy that there are principles, but the principles are not eternal. This philosophy is distinctive to Chinese civilization.

Chinese kung fu has encompassed technology, medical science, and art. These rich connotations have given birth to the most overriding concept in traditional Chinese culture: Human kind represents a small universe, while heaven, earth, and human kind constitute a harmonized whole. This understanding is also concerned with how the Chinese civilization approaches all the natural existences. Based on this theory, we can produce a number of others, such as the mutual complement of *yin* and *yang*, the harmony between *yin* and *yang*. The core philosophy about kung fu is "to guard the middle ground," which involves expessing these concepts with our bodies.

Some scholars maintain that kung fu is a philosophical notion, which also highlights kung fu's distinctive disparities from other forms of combat. Kung fu has already evolved into an ideal of Taoism due to its incorporation of technology, medical science, and art. Tao, as an encapsulation of the Oriental philosophy, is omnipresent. Western philosophy is built on logical analysis and deductive reasoning, while Chinese philosophy is more committed to studying the origin of everything and its inherent rules of evolution, which gives birth to a distinctively ethnic system of understanding nature, history, and ethics, in addition to the theory of knowledge and methodology. Based on such a philosophy, the Chinese culture is inclusive, exemplifying an openness to embrace the different and diverse.

The Chinese practice kung fu in search of Tao to enhance spiritual edification. This practice exemplifies their tireless exploration of Tao.

Looking back, I find that wave after wave of young people are marching toward this Tao of kung fu in high spirits.

Zhong Haiming

CHAPTER I

DREAM OF KUNG FU

She stamps on the otherwise still water and swoops into a boundless bamboo grove. Her graceful poise changes with the movement of swaying bamboo, just like a butterfly fluttering its wings in blossoming flowers.

He closely follows her through the thriving forest and stands tiptoe on top of a bamboo stalk, his sleeves drifting in the wind.

Both have made themselves part of the grove, sourcing power from nature and performing swift jumps and somersaults, with their swords and white gowns veiled and unveiled by the deep greens. Amid this intoxicatingly tranquil setting, they are actually fighting each other to the death.

She cannot wait to surprise all the martial artists across the country, while he insists she should take time and strengthen her spiritual cultivation first under his guidance. It is a pity that they have never agreed with each other.

The two rise into the sky, making brilliant moves with their swords and believing they are fighting for the so-called true self.

This scene featuring rivaling swordsmen in the bamboo grove is selected from the movie *Crouching Tiger, Hidden Dragon* (2000) and is suffused with orientally poetic flavors. This film constructs a dream that exploits some deep-seated sentiments and provides some never-seen-before novelty. In this dream, we are writing poems with swords; in this dream, we weigh no more than twenty-one grams; in this dream, we have discovered a graceful bamboo bridge leading to the ancient China.

In this Oriental country, everyone, whether literati or swordsmen, possesses a sincere affection for bamboo. Men of letters declare, "One can dine without meat but cannot live without bamboo. No meat in the diet makes people lose weight, but no access to bamboo in life will breed vulgarity." They are fascinated by the sounds of bamboo groves. Listening to the rustling and murmurs of bamboo can inspire them to focus on their inner voices. It is commonly known among Chinese martial artists that "bamboo grows little by little, while martial skill improves day after day." The flexible but unyielding nature of the bamboo exemplifies the overriding principle of Chinese martial artists, which values both force and softness. In the Chinese mindset, bamboo is associated with a virtuous and independent gentleman or a warrior with integrity and loyalty. It is commonly believed in China that a man with lofty bearings must be a bamboo lover.

影武者

KUNG FU
MOVIE STARS

Bruce Lee

In the 1970s, a Chinese bamboo-lover marveled the world with his kung fu performance on the wide screen. Clad in yellow sportswear, he subdued his rival who carried a pair of cudgels by dodging and wielding a slim bamboo strip with ease. He was remembered as one of the best-known kung fu stars and the icon of kung fu culture. He pioneered the worldwide revolutions of kung fu philosophy, inspired the foundation of UFC (Ultimate Fighting Championship), founded Jeet Kune Do, and was celebrated as the "Father of MMA" (mixed martial arts). His name was Bruce Lee.

Bruce Lee was born in San Francisco during World War II. The next year, he migrated back to Hong Kong with his family, shortly after which Hong Kong was seized by the Japanese troops. In his childhood, Lee once ran onto the rooftop of a three-story building, cursing the

Japanese fighter planes flying over, which indicated his courage and short temper. However, he could also be a quiet child, sometimes suddenly falling into silence and dwelling on some bizarre questions. This obsession with meditation was carried into his adulthood, when he was still fascinated with philosophical thinking. Drawing from the essential ideas of Laozi, *The Book of Changes*, Zen, Friedrich Nietzsche, Jiddu Krishnamurti, Jean-Paul Sartre, and others, he developed a distinct philosophical system on martial arts studies.

Confucius, an ancient Chinese philosopher, once remarked, "Among any three people walking, I will find something to learn for sure." Lee had many martial arts instructors. At the age of seven, Lee started to learn the Wu-style shadow boxing from his father. Later, he studied theories on the internal martial arts from Master Leung Tsz-pang, who was known for his profound knowledge in this field. At the age of thirteen, Lee had the good fortune

Bruce Lee was the best-known kung fu star. Here he performs kung fu on the set of *Enter the Dragon* (1973).

to become a student of Ip Man, one of the most famed martial arts masters, and started to learn Wing Chun in a systematic way. At seventeen, Lee won the school boxing contest with Wing Chun. Later, he built on his Wing Chun skills by incorporating merits of various schools, such as Jit-Kune, Hung Kuen, Shaolin boxing, Tam-Tuei, Choy Lee Fut, poking feet boxing, and crane boxing. He also learned judo from Japanese martial artist Taiheie and Philippine cudgel play from his disciple Dan Inosanto. In addition, he studied boxing techniques by watching Joe Louis, the legend of the boxing world, train and compete. By making brilliant use of what he learned from others, Lee succeeded in solving the mysteries of the time-honored Chinese philosophy and advocated "using no way as way, having no limitation as limitation." In 1963, *Chinese Gung Fu*, authored by Lee, was published. At the age of twenty-seven, he formally named his own boxing style "Jeet Kune Do."

Lee's kung fu moves are marked by swiftness and forcefulness. What about the underlying theories he had observed? Lee once expounded on his own philosophy on kung fu in an interview. According to him, a practitioner should "empty his mind, be formless, shapeless, like water. Water can flow, or it can crash; be water, my friend." This invisible and seemingly intangible "*qi* energy" occupies a central position in understanding eastern philosophy and Chinese kung fu. Lee's ideas accurately interpret the notion of the art of kung fu. Chinese kung fu incorporates poetic and logical approaches to see the world in a seamless way, while film is an ideal medium to present all this. The screen in the darkness builds a magical kung fu dream for us.

Kung fu movies starring Bruce Lee took the world by storm, repetitively challenging the established

1 | 2
1

1 Bruce Lee is lost in thought on the set of *Enter the Dragon* (1973).

2 Bruce Lee has become an emblem of kung fu, while nunchucks are emblematic of Bruce Lee.

conceptions of kung fu. Due to Lee's influence, nunchucks are still regarded as lethal weapons and thus it is illegal to possess or carry them in some countries or regions, where it is even legal to possess a gun or marijuana. Lee starred in a number of movies including *The Big Boss* (1971), *The Way of the Dragon* (1972), *The Chinese Connection* (1972), *Enter the Dragon* (1973), and *The Game of Death* (1972). His sudden death in 1973 threw martial arts lovers across the world into deep mourning. Twenty-seven years after his death, a documentary titled *Bruce Lee: A Warrior's Journey* (2000) caught wide attention after the release. The last forty minutes of the video feature Lee in his signature yellow jumpsuit performing Jeet Kune Do. These scenes, publicized for the first time, have brought us back to the 1970s, a decade defined by kung fu movies that celebrate the true skills of martial artists.

Though Lee was a professional martial arts instructor and actor, he was ambitious to promote martial arts philosophy. His life was short, but his influence was profound. It is because of Bruce Lee that the word "kung fu" was included in the English dictionary. Dana White, chairman of UFC, reiterated, "Bruce Lee was successful and mainstream. He was the father of mixed martial arts."

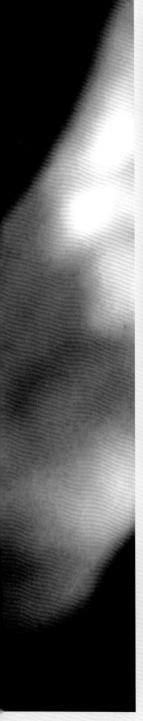

Muhammad Ali, the legendary boxer, once said, "Bruce Lee was a great person. He was the most outstanding in his field. I wish I could have had the chance to meet him, as I do love his martial arts. He is beyond his time."

Thirty years after Bruce Lee's death, the movie *Kill Bill* (2003) acted as another dream weaver for kung fu lovers. Uma Thurman sports Lee's iconic yellow jumpsuit and confronts the Crazy 88 gang, who all wear masks as Lee did in *The Green Hornet* (1966). After merciless combat, Uma stand with her yellow sportswear spotted with bloodstains and fifty-seven bodies at her feet. This breathtaking battle scene was the highlight of violence aesthetics on screen that year. Director Quentin Tarantino is known as the "disciple of Hong Kong movies." In addition to Bruce Lee movies, Tarantino is also a diehard fan of other kung fu movies of that age. *The 36th Chamber of Shaolin* (1978) starring Gordon Liu still lingering in Tarantino's memory, he invited Gordon Liu to play the characters Johnny Mo and Pai Mei in *Kill Bill*. *Kill Bill* was not only intended to pay tribute to Bruce Lee and all the outstanding kung fu movies of that age, but also to trigger nostalgic sentiments of kung fu fans across the globe.

1	2
	3

1 Bruce Lee was known for his confident look and outstanding kung fu skills. His innovations in martial arts philosophy won great admiration from kung fu practitioners across the globe.

2 *The Game of Death* (1972) was Bruce Lee's last movie.

3 The heroine in *Kill Bill* (2003) is dressed in Bruce Lee's signature jumpsuit as a tribute to Bruce Lee.

Liu Chia-liang

Gordon Liu, who played Pai Mei in *Kill Bill* (2003), started to learn Hung Kuen at the age of seven. He was only twenty-two when *The 36th Chamber of Shaolin* (1978) was produced. His impressive martial valor and kung fu skills made his martial monk character quite convincing. Liu Chia-liang, the director of this movie and also Gordon's adoptive brother, is one of the most accomplished martial arts movie directors in the world. At the age of nine, he learned martial arts from his father, Liu Cham. Liu Cham's instructor was Lin Shih-jung, who was personally instructed by Wong Fei-hung, a kung fu master of some significance in the history of Chinese kung fu. Liu Chia-liang is skilled not only in the orthodox school of Hung Kuen, but also in other varieties. His kung fu expertise is intensive and extensive.

In the 1950s, Liu Chia-liang, who was already versed in Hung Kuen, followed his father's footsteps into the film industry. At that time, social changes were resulting in enormous transformations in the lifestyles of martial artists. The big screen had evolved into a new medium to present and promote martial arts.

Kung fu movies are one of the highlights of the Hong Kong film industry. Liu's movies are marked by simple storylines and high-note kung fu performances. Unsophisticated moral values coupled with traditional customs and cultures of the area south of the Five Ridges are common elements of Liu's movies. Liu usually serves as director, playwright, choreographer and actor. He utilizes camera lenses to capture changes in poses and demonstrations of different moves, transforming battle scenes into step-by-step martial arts textbooks and presenting to the audience the defining features of different weapons and responsive solutions. In this sense, Liu's movies are even more thought-provoking than those starring Bruce Lee. In *Eighteen Legendary Weapons of China* (1982), Liu Chia-liang, Liu Chia-yung, and Gordon Liu joined hands to exhibit distinct advantages and disadvantages as well as the mutual relationships of various weapons. All the kung fu moves showcased in the movie are not groundless speculations but based on time-honored kung fu heritage in China. The director has drawn inspiration from his profound understanding of kung fu and decades-long practice in this field. In reality, kung fu training is marked by boredom, hardship, and seclusion. With his films, Liu adds some fun to this long-standing dullness. The almost self-abusive physical training and repetitive practice with tricky weapons are indispensible to the formula of kung fu movies, while the fatigue of young disciples poses sharp contrast to the leisure of the elderly instructors, adding comedic elements to movies and enabling the audience to understand the basics and training processes of various schools in an entertaining way. Director Liu is skilled in deconstructing kung fu into a recreational medium through film, exerting enormous influence on the kung fu genre.

Kung fu Master Wong Fei-hung firmly believed that a martial artist is supposed to be virtuous in the first place and should win reverence and respect for his virtues. He insisted that martial arts instructors should not hold prejudice against martial arts practitioners from other schools or against female practitioners. He was the first martial artist in China to instruct female disciples and even founded a female lion dance troupe. Wong had influenced Liu Chia-liang in a profound way. His *My*

1–2 In *Kill Bill 2* (2004), Gordon Liu plays Pai Mei.

Young Auntie (1981) was centered on a female character played by Kara Hui. At the age of twenty, Hui had proven her talent not only in drama movies but also in action movies. Her convincing performance was recognized by the Hong Kong Film Awards Committee, who granted her the Best Actress Award.

Liu Chia-liang is also attached to bamboo. San Te, the leading character in *The 36th Chamber of Shaolin*, is practicing kung fu in a bamboo grove when he is inspired by the flexibility of bamboo and thus invents a new weapon featuring a cudgel with three sections. In another scene, San Te disciplines his new disciple in a narrow alley by using long bamboo poles, demonstrating the outstanding skills of the leading character. In *Challenge of the Masters* (1976), there is a scene set in a bamboo grove, where the protagonist Wong Fei-hung subdues his rival by using bamboo to trip him after battling with him barehanded and with weapons. After subduing his rival, Wong spares his life and forgives him, which sincerely convinces his rival. *Drunken Monkey* (2003) is Liu's most recent work and also the last kung fu movie released by Shaw Brothers Studio. The old escort, played by Liu Chia-liang, is ambushed in a bamboo grove, where he climbs to the top of the bamboo like a monkey with injuries and uses the flexibility of bamboo and his *qinggong* ("light body skill") skills to escape. Liu Chia-liang, who was already sixty-six years old, was still impressive for his agility and explosive force.

It is commonly believed that *Drunken Master II* (1994) represents Liu's ultimate achievements in the film industry. This movie was selected as one of the "Best 10 Movies of the Year" by *Time* magazine. In this movie, Liu and Jackie Chan battle more than a hundred axe-wielding gangsters in a teahouse. In this scene, Liu again maximizes

the power of bamboo. Cornered by a hundred men armed with axes, Liu uses a bamboo pole as a weapon and deters the enemies upstairs while Chan wields tables and chairs downstairs to hold off the gangsters. Liu uses the pole to rescue Chan and then stamps it on staircase so forcefully that it breaks in the middle. Liu had sprayed oil on the bamboo pole and Chan's body beforehand so that Chan would not hurt himself while climbing the pole. Later, Chan wields the heavily damaged pole to keep his opponents at a distance. This battle scene with breathtaking tension was neither shot with wires nor processed with CG effects, but depended solely on the personal skills of the actors. Liu made this movie to raise money to buy offices for the Martial Artists Association, which exemplified his virtues as a martial artist. The drunken boxing moves in the movie originated from the Eight Immortals in Taoism. Therefore, Chan imitates these immortals by putting his finger to the corners of his lips, or squeezing his eyes and brows to mimic playing the flute, or poking others' eyes using the feminine gestures. These references are only intelligible to those deeply familiar with Chinese culture. Most Westerners would not pick up on the cultural connotations of these shots. But whether from the West or East, all viewers are impressed by the fabulous kung fu scenes and humorous shots. In this sense, kung fu has been transformed into an entertaining medium for cultural exchange.

1
| 2

1 Liu Chia-Liang is the most accomplished director of kung fu movies in the world.

2 *The 36th Chamber of Shaolin* (1978), a kung fu movie directed by Liu Chia-liang, features a battle between three-section cudgels and broad knives.

pages 20–21

| 2
1 | 3
| 4

1 *Return to the 36th Chamber* (1980) is a sequel to *The 36th Chamber of Shaolin*. In the movie, bamboo is closely associated with kung fu.

2-4 Gordon Liu acts as a righteous martial monk in *The 36th Chamber of Shaolin*.

Jackie Chan

After the death of Bruce Lee, kung fu fans shifted their attention to Jackie Chan. Just like Bruce Lee, Chan was also a naughty devil in his childhood. Unlike Liu Chia-liang, Chan was not instructed by kung fu masters, but learned skills in the Peking Opera troupes. Traditional Oriental opera is in essence a combination of singing, dancing, drama, pantomime, and action play. Martial arts performance in Peking Opera is ridden with danger. Any performer of this kind has to sign a waiver that declares that no one is responsible in case of an accident. In the Peking Opera troupes, Chan got up at five o'clock in the morning to practice until twelve o'clock at night. Martial arts performers are usually dressed in weighty costumes and thick-soled shoes to perform challenging actions, which requires that partners practice extensively. Therefore, these performers are quite sensitive to the exact positions of their partners during movements, which is of overriding importance to fighters in real combats. It is commonly known that having practiced kung fu for three years, you still cannot equal a martial arts performer in Peking Opera who has taken exercise for one year. Chan acquired his kung fu skills and established his distinctive style through such practice.

In 1978, Yuen Woo-ping, director of *Drunken Master* (1978), recognized Chan's talent as a comedian and thus based the character Wong Fei-hung on him. Chan incorporated humor into his impressive kung fu performance and pioneered a new genre of kung fu movies—kung fu comedies.

Benevolence and optimism are recurring themes in Chan's movies. His actions and facial expressions are reminiscent of Charlie Chaplin. One cannot help laughing at the first sight of Chan. These humorous elements downplay the violence in *Drunken Master* and make it a comedy that appeals to all ages. The characters that Chan has played are mostly kindhearted young men who love kung fu but resent violence. Actually, all his characters encapsulate a basic expectation that martial arts instructors have of their disciples—virtue. As his movies gained more and more popularity, Jackie Chan was showered with honors and awards. He has been celebrated as an international star. Chan is an enthusiastic philanthropist and proponent of public welfare. His generosity is another exemplification of his virtues as a

martial artist. Today, Chan still has an active presence in kung fu movies. He knows that his success is built on the inexhaustible magic of kung fu.

Kung fu lovers saw their dreams realized in 2008, when Jackie Chan and Jet Li joined hands to construct a kung fu dream for the first time. In the movie *The Forbidden Kingdom*, Chan and Li play a monk and a Taoist priest respectively. A line from this movie defines kung fu: "*Gongfu* (Chinese *pinyin* for "kung fu") is hard work over time. A painter can have *gongfu*. Or the butcher who cuts meat every day with such skill . . . his knife never touches bone. Nothing is softer than water . . . yet it can overcome rock. It does not fight. It flows around the opponent. Formless, nameless . . . the true master dwells within. Only you can free him."

The Forbidden Kingdom is laden with established components of classic kung fu movies, including chasing in the bamboo grove and crossing the river on a bamboo raft. Kung fu moves showcased in this movie include drunken boxing, shadow boxing, mantis boxing, floating on water, cudgel play, and tricky weapons. The audience cannot help but be awe-stricken when Chan and Li fight each other, and both deserve reverence and respect for their glorious professional careers. The shots featuring "thirteen monks rescuing the deity" and Li playing the monk remind the audience of Li's classic kung fu movie *Shaolin Temple* (1982).

1	2
	3
	4
	5

1 Jackie Chan plays the young Wong Fei-hung, who is naughty and energetic in *Drunken Master* (1978).

2-5 *Fearless Hyena* (1979) is the first kung fu movie for which Jackie Chan worked as the director, playwright, and choreographer.

Jet Li

Born in Beijing in 1963, Jet Li was admitted to the Beijing Sports School at the age of seven and has been arduously training in kung fu ever since. In 1972, Li won the Outstanding Performance Award in a folk martial arts contest at the age of nine. Li reached the climax at the Fourth National Sports Meeting in 1979, when he claimed five gold medals with impressive perseverance despite injuries. Even his competitors burst into tears for him. His success was a reward for the pain he had endured and the sweat he had shed.

In 1982, Li's first movie, *Shaolin Temple*, was released. Young martial artist Jet Li immediately rose to fame. In the early 1980s, a movie ticket cost only a dime in China, but the total box office amounted to 140 million yuan. Decades later, *Shaolin Temple* is still a legend to several generations. Chieh Yuan, the martial monk played by Li, was an icon of that age.

Ever since, Li, known as the "kung fu emperor," has played many other kung fu heroes. As a young man, he soon established himself as a miraculous incarnation of Chinese kung fu in both America and Europe and a much-sought-after superstar worldwide.

In recent years, Li has found inner peace in the Buddhist domain. Three decades ago, he was a Shaolin martial monk on the screen. Today, he has transformed into an adherent of Buddhism. He was quoted as saying, "Buddhist practice has changed my personality and life, enabling me to approach everything with openness and tolerance." There seems to be a subtle connection between his life and his movies. On the screen, he portrays kung fu heroes who are keen to help the underprivileged. In real life, he is fully committed to public welfare and has founded a charity to provide relief to victims of natural disasters and youth suffering from mental problems. He deserves the title of a modern swordsman.

1
2 | 3

1 Jackie Chan performed drunken boxing in the movie *The Forbidden Kingdom* (2008).

2 Jackie Chan and Jet Li battle in *The Forbidden Kingdom*.

3 Jet Li rose to fame in the 1980s. *Shaolin Temple* (1982) is his first and best-known movie.

宗师魂

KUNG FU INSTRUCTORS

Shaolin Temple

The Southern and Northern Shaolin Temples are always shrouded with mysteries, just like two deities who live in the mountains and observe the mortal world with mercy. They have witnessed prosperity and also survived flames of war. In the early Sui dynasty, the Northern Shaolin Temple was burned to ashes by peasant rebels. In the Qing dynasty, Emperor Yongzheng issued an imperial decree to destroy the Southern Shaolin Temple. In the early years of the Republican era, Northern Shaolin Temple was again victimized, with a large number of structures torched. After the foundation of PRC, Shaolin Temple barely survived the social-political turbulence in the 1960s and early 1970s. Nowadays, the Shaolin Temples have been almost restored to their original glamour and glory, but have started to be troubled by their fame. Endless streams of tourists have disturbed the tranquility of the temples. What has happened to the Shaolin Temples is a testament to the Buddhist proverb "Everything is ever changing. Only through nirvana can we gain eternal happiness."

Toward the end of the Sui dynasty, thirteen martial monks from Shaolin Temple participated in the rebellion against the ruthless Sui rulers at the invitation of the later Emperor Taizong of Tang, Li Shimin. Their involvement had accelerated the foundation of the Tang dynasty. The kung fu skills of the thirteen cudgel monks have become legend. Following Tang, Shaolin boxing took in the strengths of various schools and the Shaolin boxing book was composed. In the Song dynasty, the Shaolin Temples attached more importance to martial arts, and lay disciples were also admitted. Whether legendary warriors or renowned military generals, their achievements were all connected with the Shaolin Temples in one way or another. In the Ming dynasty, Japanese pirates disturbed

Songshan Shaolin Temple is a holy place for numerous kung fu fans.

the southeastern Chinese coastline, where civilians began to live in endless panic. The local officials had no choice but to turn to the Shaolin Temples. Shaolin monks rose to the occasion and headed to the Chinese borders with iron cudgels in hand. After fierce battles with these pirates, all the martial monks sacrificed their lives and left a tragic and awe-inspiring chapter in Chinese history. After the establishment of Qing and the racial slaughters and ethnic discrimination by the Qing army, warriors who were determined to restore the Ming regime trained their followers in Shaolin Temples to resist Qing's rule. Later, the Southern Shaolin Temple was encircled and charred by the Qing government.

Since Bodhidharma crossed the river on a reed leaf, generations of Shaolin monks have practiced martial arts in the mountains in the company of gurgling springs and moonlight to gain understanding of the truth about life. It might seem puzzling that traditional Chinese martial arts have originated from the Buddhist domain, which values peace and resents violence. However, Buddhists have no difficulty explaining this, because martial art is also about humanity and virtues; there is an inseverable tie between Buddhist temples and the mortal world.

Movies on Shaolin kung fu were all best sellers in the 1970s and 1980s. Representative works in these decades include *Five Shaolin Masters* (1974), *The Shaolin Avengers* (1976), *Challenge of the Masters* (1976), *Executioners from Shaolin* (1977), *Two Champions of Shaolin* (1980), *Shaolin Temple* (1982), *Shaolin Temple II: Kids from Shaolin* (1984), and *Martial Arts of Shaolin* (1986). For years, the vicissitudes of Shaolin Temples have been presented to a wide audience through the big screen. Martial arts actors and directors active in the kung fu movie industry are not only dream weavers for the magical and mysterious Shaolin kung fu but also passionate recorders of legendary kung fu masters from Shaolin Temples.

Quanzhou Shaolin Temple prospered in the Hongwu period in Ming and collapsed in the Qianlong period in Qing. It was not restored until 1992.

Wong Fei-hung

Wong Fei-hung was recognized as the epitome of
Southern Shaolin kung fu. Born in 1847, Wong was not
only a heavily-acclaimed kung fu master but also a well-
respected doctor who considered it his duty to save lives,
relieve pains, and help the underprivileged. Wong started
his training in martial arts at the age of six under the
instruction of his father, Wong Kei-ying, who was known
as one of the "Ten Tigers of Guangdong" in late Qing. At
the age of thirteen, Wong Fei-hung had learned everything
his father had to offer. After this, he traveled across the
country to learn from renowned kung fu instructors,
followed their instructions, and trained himself arduously,
until he became a master himself. Versed in tiger-style
moves in Hung Kuen, he was thus known as "Tiger
Maniac" among martial artists. He was also skilled in lion
dancing, a unique form of folk art integrating various kung
fu styles. Therefore, he was also known as "Lion King." In
addition to his achievements in martial arts, Wong was an

accomplished doctor as well, who had no rival in dealing
with fractures and other physical injuries.

Wong was greatly admired and revered by later
generations, not only for his sobriquets but also his noble
characters and tragic life story. In his adolescence, Wong
was commonly recognized for his passion to deliver
justice and his courage to punish vice in his hometown.
Even ruffians and gangsters would behave themselves
before him out of fear of his kung fu skills. In 1894, Wong
joined the army to fight against the Japanese invaders in
Taiwan at the age of forty-seven. He fought in hundreds
of battles until Taiwan was finally lost to Japan. After
shedding blood in real wars, Wong started to question
whether kung fu skills were effective on the battlefield. As
a military surgeon, he realized that violence can always
cause injuries. Therefore, after returning to his hometown,
he shifted his focus to his medical career and declared
that he would no longer take disciples or teach kung fu.
However, in 1911, at the age of sixty-four, Wong resumed
his career as a martial artist and served as the chief trainer
in the civilian corps in Guangdong. In the following years,

1 Foshan Wong Fei-hung Memorial Hall. Wong was highly skilled in lion dance and was thus known as "Lion King."

2 The Hung gar gung ji subduing tiger fist manual created by Wong Fei-hung.

3 The exterior of Foshan Wong Fei-hung Memorial Hall.

4 The interior of Foshan Wong Fei-hung Memorial Hall.

he was keen to stand for justice, using his kung fu skills. He was a household name in Guangzhou for his chivalrous deeds. In 1919, one of Wong's sons, a promising martial artist, was shot to death after being framed. Years later, Wong's clinic, to which he was fully committed all his life, was burned to ashes. Stricken by these blows and haunted by depression and frustration, Wong died in sickness the next year at the age of seventy-seven.

Wong was a noble and chivalrous martial artist in every sense. He spent his life helping others with his kung fu skills and medical knowledge. He came to the rescue of the underpriviliged when they were bullied and suppressed, relieved his patients of pains, and stood up to defend his country when it was thrown into danger. His life experience encapsulated sufferings of the Chinese people at his age. The Chinese nation was plagued with turbulence and tribulation from late Qing to the early Republican era; what had happened to Wong was universal to the majority of Chinese people at the time. This partly explains why later generations tend

to commemorate him in movies. There are more than a hundred Chinese films portraying Wong in addition to numerous soap operas. Over twenty actors have played him. He has already evolved into a cultural icon and phenomenon. Among all these actors, Jet Li is best recognized. In 1991, Li was invited by director Tsui Hark to star in *Once upon a Time in China* (1991). Tsui wrote the story and script himself and utilized a new approach to depict a well-known martial artist. His movie is defined by a fresh perspective, elaborate production, and poetic atmosphere. The battle scenes in the film are meticulously designed with a distinctive concept. Tsui had accurately captured Wong's prestige and personality, his kung fu performance marked not only with valor but also with subtlety. This movie is celebrated as one of the classics of the 1990s and is still a hotly discussed topic among film lovers. Movies on Wong are mostly produced in Hong Kong. By now, Wong, as a historical figure, has become one of the components of Hong Kong culture and an iconic celebrity for all Chinese.

1   3
2

1–2 Jet Li plays Wong Fei-hung in *Once upon a Time in China* (1991). His handsome and tough look as well as his outstanding kung fu skills made him the best star to play Wong Fei-hung.

3 Kwan Tak-hing played Wong Fei-hung in more movies than any other actor. Kwan, at the age of seventy-three, performed complicated kung fu actions in the movie *Magnificent Butcher* (1979).

Ip Man

The Southern Shaolin Temple was burned to ashes by the Qing rulers but its disciples who survived this disaster started to popularize kung fu in Fujian, Guangdong, and other areas where kung fu practice was a common profession. Among various schools, the non-mainstream Wing Chun was the most eye-catching practice.

Wing Chun, as a branch of the Southern Shaolin school, has no chief instructor or integral management system. It has nothing to do with dragon dancing or lion dancing, and the practitioners do not represent the Wing Chun school in public events. Yim Wing-chun, founder of Wing Chun, started to learn kung fu from Master Ng Mui at an early age. Ng Mui once came across a snake fighting with a crane, from which she suddenly realized the underlying principles of boxing and passed the art on to her student. On basis of these principles, Yim Wing-chun came up with a systematic set of boxing. Director Yuen Woo-ping's movie *Wing Chun* (1994) is based on her experience and stars Michelle Yeoh and Donnie Yen as the legendary Yim Wing-chun and her husband.

To practice Wing Chun, the disciples have to pair up with their instructors and practice lengthy Chi Sau (sticky hands) drills. Therefore, one instructor can take in only a limited number of disciples, and only young men born in wealthy families have access to Wing Chun, as the tuition is relatively high. Ip Man is one of the lucky boys. He was the last disciple of Chan Wah-shun and started to learn from Chan at the age of seven. Ip was born in Foshan, Guangdong, in 1893, when China was in the throes of radical changes. These social changes had challenged traditional thoughts and beliefs, throwing people into

conflict. Ip was profoundly inspired by traditional Confucian teaching and headed to Hong Kong to study at sixteen. There he had to adapt to Western educational systems and values that were unfamiliar to him. The sharp contrast between East and West made clear the problems of the country and spurred him to search for a solution. By chance, Ip became acquainted with Leung Big, son of Leung Jan who was a master of Wing Chun, in Hong Kong. In his free time, Ip started to practice Wing Chun with Big, who spared no effort to teach him all that he himself had learned. *The Legend Is Born: Ip Man*, released in 2010, depicts Ip Man's childhood and his adolescent years. The actor To Yu-hang, a martial arts champion, brought the

character of young Ip Man to life.

With the foundation of a Republican nation, the whole society had taken on a new look. However, such a thriving scene did not last long before the Japanese invaders dragged China into a war that lasted for eight years. The Japanese took control of Foshan in 1938, when Ip found that the kung fu skills he learned throughout life were useless in modern wars. Therefore, Ip started to question whether there was any practical meaning for martial artists to stick to traditional kung fu.

In 2008, Donnie Yen starred in the movie *Ip Man*, which closely associates the master's life experience with his social context. This movie is largely based on Ip's true life experiences, such as bending a pistol with a single thumb, capturing robbers, and defeating the Japanese warriors with ease.

In 1949, Ip, serving as the interim director of police under the rule of the Nationalist Government of the Republic of China, sought refuge in Hong Kong due to power changes. The social changes in the larger context had enabled Ip to obtain a better understanding of his own values. He resumed his boxing instruction career, which led to the popularization and further development of Wing Chun in Hong Kong. The movie *Ip Man 2: Legend of the Grandmaster* (2010) depicts Ip's experience of taking disciples in Hong Kong. In this movie, Ip and Hung Chunnam stage an exciting contest on a round table using Wing Chun and Hung Kuen respectively. This scene enabled Sammo Hung to win a Hong Kong Film Award for Best Action Choreography for the second time. Donnie Yen, who plays Ip in the movie, is the most active kung fu star in recent years. Yen started to learn kung fu at an early age and scored glorious achievements in the Hong Kong

and Hollywood film industries. He is the action director for *Flash Point* (2007), which has been acclaimed for containing the most realistic combats and thus won the World Stunt Awards—Best Action in a Foreign Language Film.

In 2013, Wong Kar-wai presented *The Grandmaster*, for which he had been preparing for years after visiting the chief instructors of Eight Grand Schools through the introduction of Wu Bin. He adopted a unique perspective to narrate the legendary life of Ip. The lines in the movie are another highlight in addition to the exquisite Northern and Southern boxing performances. One of the inspiring lines reads, "Some people are respected, while others are forgotten. No matter what, all of them have to resign to fate." It is certain that Ip was not the only master in the world. He was greatly respected, while others who were equally respectable were forgotten. All is predetermined by fate.

Three movies on Ip Man and Wing Chun have been produced. These movies tell us the complex life experience and changing thoughts of Ip, a kung fu master of his age. Wing Chun, originally unknown to the majority, was popularized by Ip and his disciples, bringing the combat strategies and expertise of this traditional Chinese martial art to kung fu lovers around the world.

2   3

1

1 Ip Man had popularized Wing Chun across the globe.

2 Ip Man does hand exercises with his disciple Bruce Lee.

3 Ip Man and his disciple Bruce Lee.

pages 36–37

1

2
3

1 Ip Chun, son of Ip Man, plays a Wing Chun master named Liang Bi in *The Legend Is Born: Ip Man* (2010), in which To Yu-hang plays Ip Man.

2 Donnie Yen plays the hero in *Ip Man* (2008).

3 Tony Leung plays Ip Man in *The Grandmaster* (2013).

Huo Yuanjia

Huo Yuanjia, twenty-five years older than Ip, was commonly recognized as a kung fu master in North China. Huo was born in 1868 in a kung fu family whose male members were all skilled practitioners of lost track boxing. He was a delicate boy and his father thus disallowed him to practice kung fu. However, he observed his father and older brothers practice kung fu and exercised in secret until he grasped what was essential to lost track boxing. In the late Qing dynasty, when China was troubled with domestic strife and foreign aggressions, the Chinese people were already aware of the nation's underdevelopment compared to Western countries. They were desperate for social change but haunted by a complex anxiety at the same time. Some of them even became concerned that Westerners might be genetically superior to East Asian people. Huo believed that practicing kung fu was effective in building up physical strength. In order to prove that physique is determined by training rather than by racial factors, he challenged Europeans of unusual strength several times, but no one dared take up his challenge. In 1910, Huo founded the Chin Woo Athletic Association in the belief that in order to promote Chinese kung fu, martial artists had to exploit the strengths of various schools in a nondiscriminatory way. Huo had led his disciples to defy the humiliating title "Sick Man of East Asia," with which the Westerners had labeled the Chinese.

Chin Woo publications have documented Huo's death. Huo was invited to dinner after defeating Japanese judo practitioners. At dinner, a Japanese doctor claimed that he had a miraculous remedy for Huo's chronic cough. Huo took the pills the doctor offered. Shortly after, Huo's health deteriorated rapidly. Soon, Huo passed away at the age of forty-two. Later, his acquaintances had his prescriptions tested and found that the pills from the Japanese doctor would gradually cause ulcers to the lungs.

Decades later, there are sixty Chin Woo branches across the globe, with a membership exceeding 400,000. The movie *Fearless* (2006) tells the story of Huo and involved the participation of outstanding martial artists from all over the world, including Thai boxing champion Somluck Kamsing, Australian wrestler Nathan Jones, German fencing expert Brandon Rhea, as well as Chinese kung fu actors Collin Chou and Chen Zhihui. Jet Li, who plays Huo in this movie, won the Hong Kong Film Award for Best Actor for his acting and kung fu skills.

Generations of Chinese sigh over Huo's tragic death, and they are partly appeased by an invented character named Chen Zhen. In 1972, Ni Kuang, a renowned writer, wrote the screenplay for *The Chinese Connection* at the invitation of Bruce Lee, in which he invented "Chen Zhen," one of the most accomplished disciples of Huo. This movie tells how Chen took revenge for his instructor Huo. Bruce Lee, for the first time, displayed his outstanding nunchucks skills on the screen. The combat scenes were shot using a realistic approach, with no stuntman used. Such an approach exerted a profound influence on the

1 2

3

1-2 Huo Yuanjia and
an early published
edition of the lost
track boxing manual.

3 Foshan Chin Woo
Athletic Association
was founded more
than one century
ago.

films that would follow it.

In 1994, the movie *Fist of Legend*, a remake of *The Chinese Connection* starring Jet Li, was released. The action choreographer Yuen Woo-ping joined efforts with Jet Li, elevating kung fu movies to a new level. The action, timing, and pacing are flawless, and Chinese martial arts are approached from a philosophical perspective. At the end of the movie, Chen rivals with a Japanese warrior who is much taller and stronger. Their contest highlights how Chinese kung fu values defeating a powerful opponent with a weak force, and demonstrates the unrestrained nature of Jeet Kune Do. This movie has been enshrined as a benchmark for action aesthetics and a milestone in the international kung fu film industry.

In 2010, Donnie Yen played Chen Zhen in *Legend of the Fist: The Return of Chen Zhen*, which could be regarded as the sequel to *Fist of Legend*. In this movie, Chen, as an immigrant worker, survives World War I in Europe. After his return to Shanghai, Chen launches overt and covert wars against the Japanese militarist forces. Yen performs both traditional Chinese kung fu and free fighting in the film. The director infuses a breath of romanticism into the character by giving him an identity as a pianist and a dangerously romantic relationship. In the night fights, Chen dresses in the black clothes Bruce Lee wore in *The Green Hornet* (1966), and the white costume Chen wears in the duel was the one Lee was clad in in the movie *The Chinese Connection*. If *Fearless* was intended to pay a tribute to Master Huo, then the three movies on Chen Zhen were actually a continuation of the Chin Woo values. All these movies are concerned with the choices of traditional martial artists in a larger social context. Just as Lu Xun said, "This choice is about life or death. This is why we call our age 'The Great Time.'"

1	3
2	4
	5

1–2 In the movie *Fearless* (2006), Huo Yuanjia, played by Jet Li, battles with outstanding martial artists around the world.

3–5 Three outstanding martial artists respectively played Chen Zhen, in *The Chinese Connection* (1972, Bruce Lee); *Fist of Legend* (1994, Jet Li); and *Legend of Fist: the Return of Chen Zhen* (2010, Donnie Yen). The first movie of the three was shot nearly four decades earlier than the last one.

侠客行

SWORDSMEN
IN MOVIES

The movie *Kung Fu Hustle* (2004) turned out to be a blockbuster. The movie delivers the following message to the audience: As long as one follows his conscience, he will become stronger. The director has simply defined "strength" by equating it with the acquisition of outstanding kung fu skills. All the masters in the movie live ordinary lives. They might be porters, tailors, peddlers, or even your landlord. They never boast about their kung fu but will always rise to the occasion at a critical time and even sacrifice their lives to deliver justice. In this sense, *Kung Fu Hustle* is more like the so-called swordsman movie and loaded with "chivalry" elements.

Dragon (2011) tells the story of a detective who is versed in martial arts, digs into an ordinary homicide case, and unveils hidden gangster strife. This experimental and artistic movie deals with action from a new perspective.

Combat is portrayed in an anatomic way so that the audience can easily identify the subtle interactions between different energy meridians, bones, blood vessels, and acupuncture points. In this sense, this movie is more like a kung fu movie, as it is closely concerned with the subtle deconstruction of kung fu.

Actually, there is no distinct boundary between kung fu movies and swordsman movies. The two overlap and complement each other. The former was primarily produced in Hong Kong, while the latter originated from Shanghai; the former is focused on the demonstration and deconstruction of kung fu but is embedded with chivalry at the same time, while the latter is more concerned with the storyline and the display of chivalry, though it is inevitably related to kung fu.

The earliest document of "swordsmen" in China

Donnie Yen plays an outstanding martial artist living in seclusion in the movie *Dragon* (2011).

dates back to the pre-Qin times more than 2,200 years ago, when China was uniform in virtues and values but divided in territory. Back then, there was no significant exclusiveness, which determined that individuals with varied beliefs and impressive competence were accepted and admired. This large context bred chivalry. It was an integral component of the Confucian, Mohist, and Taoist thought systems. With the passage of time, "chivalry" has taken on richer meanings. Anyone keen to enforce justice, perform his duties, keep his promise, value loyalty, and be benevolent in nature is taken to be an incarnation of chivalry. "Swordsman" refers to not only a profession but also a special life attitude and ethos in the Chinese mindset. Batman, Spider-Man, and Iron Man are all identified as "swordsmen" by the Chinese. In pre-Qin times, philosophers were active, and swordsmen freely traveled across the country to live up to their ambitions. It was a golden age featuring thriving culture and a burst of various teachings. In this context, fully developed martial arts culture came into shape. The Chinese character for "martial art" indicates that martial art is intended as a method to put an end to violence. In this age, martial arts combined with chivalry, evolving into an integral whole. Liang Yusheng, a writer renowned for swordsman fiction, once remarked that "chivalry is the soul, while martial art is the body; chivalry is the purpose, while martial art is the means to achieve chivalry."

The Chinese dream of the swordsman finds its origin in literature. Biographies from the pre-Qin times to Han, poems in Sui and Tang, tales in Tang and Song, and novels in Ming and Qing—all these literary forms had built upon chivalry. In the Republican era, the swordsman novelist Xiang Kairan was a martial artist himself, while another novelist, Li Shanji, was also fascinated with *qigong* (a

The One-Armed Swordsman (1967), directed by Chang Cheh, is marked with solemnity, pioneering the neo-swordsman movie. The young swordsman Fang Kang, played by Jimmy Wang Yu, is convincing and memorable.

system of deep breathing exercises). They were not only novelists but also theorists. Jin Yong, Liang Yusheng, and Gu Long, who gained fame in the latter half of the twentieth century, all drew inspiration from swordsman literature in the Republican era. But they were more focused on characters' personalities and sentiments, and also their destinies. Swordsman literature is commonly adapted into soap operas and films, giving birth to a diversified swordsman culture.

The swordsman genre is a signature of the Chinese film industry. *Young Heroes*, shot in Shanghai in 1927, has been regarded as the first of this category. Later, this genre would be popular among audiences, but within thirty years of the foundation of PRC, no more movies of this genre were produced in Mainland China, while Hong Kong and Taiwan directors started to play a prominent role in this field. In the 1960s, Hong Kong movie companies such as Shaw Brothers Studio produced a number of classical swordsman movies, which are still hotly sought after today.

In 1967, *The One-Armed Swordsman*, directed by Chang Cheh, turned out to be a huge success. This movie depicts a swordsman named Fang Kang, who loses his right arm and finds himself haunted by one misfortune after another. His life is ridden with various conflicts and complex sentimental issues such as resentment and gratitude. He is always caught in the middle and thus questions whether he should retreat into a secluded life or play an active role in society. He has to make difficult choices all the time. Every time, he follows his heart. The movie presents to the audience a swordsman's inner world, which is marked with solemnity and simplicity, in a thought-provoking narrative style.

The One-Armed Swordsman pioneered a new trend in swordsman movies. It is intended to encourage self-affirmation, self-education, and self-motivation. Forty-four years later, Jimmy Wang Yu, who played the leading role in this movie, played a ruthless gangster leader who displays menacing valor in Dragon. At the age of sixty-seven, Wang Yu was still in such good shape that he made an impressive performance by fully capturing the defining features of Hung Kuen and Heng Lian kung fu. The lead character, Liu Jinxi, played by Donnie Yen, cuts off one of his own arms, an obvious tribute to The One-Armed Swordsman. However, The One-Armed Swordsman is focused on loyalty, while Dragon is more concerned with betrayal. However, betrayal of bygone vices and evil forces is equal in loyalty to lofty character.

We can never talk about a swordsman without mentioning his milieu, which is commonly referred to as jianghu (literally translated as "rivers and lakes"). Jianghu can be the whole society, a swordsman's secluded residence, or his secretive sub-community that observes distinctive principles varied from those in the mainstream political systems. Anyway, jianghu is where a swordsman lives.

Director Chor Yuen has a special attachment to veteran swordsmen whose adolescent ambitions have already worn away with the passage of time, giving way to profound reflections. Chor is skilled in capturing characters' inner worlds and the dramatic storylines and glamorous settings create tranquil and classic atmospheres. His movie Killer Clans (1976) depicts a swordsman clan that is fraught with complexity and peril. At last, the righteous swordsman secedes from the clan and accompanies his lover to a distant land, saying farewell to his so-called bosom friends who did not deserve his trust. This movie was adapted from Gu Long's novel, which define chivalry as prioritization of love over power. A swordsman lives up to chivalry to seek spiritual consolation in an unfair social context. If jianghu operates on the basis of power struggles instead of morality and justice, the swordsman will find no meaning in life.

It is the writer-director King Hu who has introduced the swordsman movie into the artistic domain. In Come Drink with Me, directed by Hu in 1966, a swordswoman lands herself in peril in order to save her older brother. Whenever her life is threatened, a drunken swordsman with a green bamboo pole in hand comes to her rescue. The director carefully considered the costumes, props, and settings in this movie. Hu also utilized the exciting drumbeats of traditional operas for rhythmic effect, and achieved an unprecedented visual effect through accurate editing, elevating the swordsman movie to a higher, more artistic level. The swordswoman Golden Swallow, played by Cheng Pei-pei, is pretty and innocent and fights in a graceful way like a dancer, becoming a classic on the wide screen. In 1971's A Touch of Zen, the swordswoman slaughters her enemies in a bamboo grove marked by Oriental aesthetics. Hu used distinctive shooting perspectives and flowing editing to create a combat scene suffused with classic and poetic flavors and an intense tempo. Known for the brilliant use of Oriental and aesthetic elements, Hu's movies are exemplary in creation of atmosphere. Scenes in his films share atmospheric similarities with ancient Chinese ink paintings. Outdoor scenes were mostly shot in secluded locations with an ancient flavor. It seems that only locations with thick historical and poetic flavor are adequate to construct his individual worlds. Built on meditations over Confucian,

1 3
2 4

1-2 Swordsman
movies such as
*Come Drink with
Me* (1966) and *A
Touch of Zen* (1971)
have contributed
memorable swords-
woman characters
to the genre.

3-4 Swordswomen
in *House of Flying
Daggers* (2004)
and *Ashes of Time*
(1994). After King
Hu, swordswomen
have evolved into
an indispensible
ingredient for
swordsman movies.

Buddhist, and Taoist thoughts, Hu's movies always dig deep into the Chinese swordsman culture. In 1975, *A Touch of Zen* was nominated for the Golden Palm Best Picture at the Cannes Film Festival and won the Technical Grand Prize Award. To some extent, this movie also provides the world with a window into ancient China.

A swordsman has to be free in the first place. In other words, all he does is to deliver freedom. But he always finds himself in a harsh reality in which he has no choice. In 1990, Hu joined hands with Tsui Hark on the movie *Swordsman*, which was adapted from Jin Yong's novel bearing the same name. In the original novel, two chief masters belong to two distinct and irreconcilable schools, but they befriend each other out of a common love for music. Therefore, the two decided to withdraw from *jianghu* to stay away from factional strife and spend the rest of their life indulging in music. However,

both are ruthlessly executed by their community. A young swordsman named Linghu Chong witnesses their tragedies and decides that he would also die for freedom. Even though he has experienced many hardships due to his unrestrained nature, he will not compromise his beliefs and finally becomes a free swordsman. The finished movie was hotly sought after for its combination of Hu's classic flavor and Tsui's imaginative power. Coupled with exquisite kung fu performance and rhythmic music, it was established as an iconic swordsman movie in the 1990s.

Seven Swords (2005), directed by Tsui Hark, displays the swordsmen's courage and willingness to shoulder responsibilities. This movie was adapted from Liang Yusheng's novel and is set in the early years of Qing, when the Manchurian rulers enforced shaved heads and literary inquisition in order to consolidate their regime. In addition, the government also banned practicing kung fu

and slaughtered martial artists one by one until "martial villages," whose mission was to pass down and popularize martial arts heritage, were about to be wiped out. In this critical situation, seven swordsmen carrying seven swords on their backs came to the rescue unexpectedly. They confronted the Qing troops and defended their ideals by shedding blood and sacrificing their lives.

In selecting shooting locations, roadhouses in the wilderness are favorable to swordsman movie directors. In 1967, King Hu directed *Dragon Inn*, which was a breakthrough for the genre. In this movie, swordsmen rival with villains in a confined space, using their wisdom and martial skills to rescue the descendants of wronged loyal officials. With the escalation of conflicts, the small roadhouse brims with intensity to the extent of explosion. Finally, all the dwellers exit the building to have a duel in the vastness. *Dragon Inn* is celebrated as a milestone of Chinese film history. However, due to technical limitations back then, directors in later generations could still find great room for improvement. In 1992, Tsui supervised a

remake of *Dragon Inn*, which could be read as a summary of the new swordsman movie genre. The shooting process coincided with the burst of outstanding Hong Kong and Taiwan actors, while the shooting techniques have also experienced significant improvements. Tsui made full use of his imaginative power while staying true to the framework of *Dragon Inn*, making a lively and funny depiction of the swordsmen's romance and integrating highly creative kung fu scenes, which explains this movie's lasting prominence. In 2011, Tsui and Jet Li joined efforts to present *Flying Swords of Dragon Gate* with 3D techniques, which was an extension of the new *Dragon Inn* story. The movie starts with a panoramic view of a grand ship manufacturer in Ming, where the swordsman played by Jet Li and the eunuch played by Gordon Liu stage a fierce battle on a ship. With the advancement of plots, various forces again met in the Dragon Inn, where they relived the classic scenes. *Flying Swords of Dragon Gate* was known for its exquisite costumes, just like a fashion show in Ming. The movie showcases the culture and customs of Ming while the impressive 3D techniques make the swordsman's world more visually striking. But what leaves an imprint on our mind is still the enduring swordsman's chivalry.

In the film *Crouching Tiger, Hidden Dragon* (2000), a man clad in a white gown, with a graceful bearing and a smile that plays at the corners of his lips, leads his horse in an unfamiliar Southern China town and walks in an unhurried manner. He acts in a refined and modest way, posing a sharp contrast to the stereotyped swordsman with an unrestrained nature. He is Li Mu Bai. Director Ang Lee drew upon King Hu's styles, observed the swordsman community from a literary perspective, and pointed to its essence by accurately imaging the swordsman, the female armed escort, the household guards, the prince, the constable, the capital officer, and the bandits in the Western regions to provide an overview of the swordsmen's world. Jen acts like a well-educated lady in daytime but turns into a burglar at night. Her unruliness and ambitions manifest both positive and negative elements of human nature. The swordswoman Yu Xiulian is a typical Chinese character. She observes the rules and strives to preserve others' dignity; she is brilliant and determined, skilled in martial arts, but surprisingly feminine to the core. She longs for a stable romantic relationship and a family. She had waited for Li Mu Bai until Jen broke into her world and shattered her dream. Li's behavior is exemplary of what is expected from a swordsman. He has a refined manner typical of a man of letters but is shrouded in mysteries. The movie has also brilliantly captured a middle-aged swordsman's struggle between sentimental longings and established moralities.

Kung fu performance in *Crouching Tiger, Hidden Dragon* presents the ultimate dream of swordsmen in the literati's mind. Fleeing and chasing on the wall at night, crowd fights in the inn, combats in the escort agency, sword play in the bamboo grove—all these scenes are unforgettable. Kung fu moves have been translated into an expression of the swordsman's personality, suffused with a solemn and antique flavor. The overwhelming green color in the movie is simultaneously seemingly unrestrained and occasionally self-contained. Lee has successfully attracted the audience with this green bamboo grove. Through complex interactions between long-standing feuds and fundamental human emotions, the director has explored the characters on a profound level. In the end, Mu Bai was poisoned to death to protect Jen. The swordsman stages a romantic tragedy that ends with self-destruction. On his deathbed, he confesses to Xiulian his secret admiration for her: "I would rather be a ghost, drifting by your side . . . as a condemned soul . . . than enter heaven without you. Because of your love . . . I will never be a lonely spirit." These last words are so poetic that they challenge our understandings of swordsmen who would embrace death with heroic valor. To our great regret, he says farewell to his beloved. Mu Bai's death could be interpreted as the return of an accomplished Taoist to the mortal world, while Jen, who jumped off the cliff, was seeking a real escape from the mortal world after attaining sudden enlightenment.

The appearance of swordsmen infuses a special charm into kung fu dreams. Though swordsmen differ from ordinary people in terms of lifestyle, they are also haunted by common dilemmas. They also keep on questioning. With the disappearance of the swordsman age, and the loss of swordsman chivalry, this spiritual appeal that had endured for thousands of years turns out to be more valuable and alluring.

A scene in the movie *Seven Swords* (2005); the heroic conducts of the swordsmen have touched all the audience.

pages 50–51

1	2
	3
	4

1–4 *Dragon Inn* (1967) with a nostalgic flavor, *New Dragon Inn* (1996) with brilliant concepts, and *Flying Swords of Dragon Gate* (2011) with magnificent visual effects have constructed interesting contrasts. Forty-four years apart between the first one and the last one, these three movies have captured different zeitgeists.

天地人

KUNG FU
PHILOSOPHY

Li Mu Bai in the movie *Crouching Tiger, Hidden Dragon* belonged to the Wudang sect. Zhang Sanfeng, in late Yuan and early Ming, was the founder of Wudang boxing. His martial arts achievements, personality, and miraculous longevity are all documented by official historians. Martial artists after Zhang made constant innovations by learning from other sects, giving birth to a distinct sect featuring inclusiveness and profundity. Wudang boxing, also known as internal martial arts, values "subduing the activity with serenity; conquering the unyielding with the yielding." It is celebrated as the representative martial arts of South China, the equivalent of the Shaolin sect in North China.

Wudang Mountain is also known as the "Divine Mountain." More than eighteen centuries ago, Taoist priests started to practice Taoism here. Later, it gradually evolved into a Taoist shrine and was held in high esteem by emperors in feudal China. Wudang Mountain was blessed with fortunes in contrast to Shaolin temples, which were damaged repeatedly. Of course, equally fortunate were the practitioners who had occupied themselves with meditations and martial trainings.

The largest martial arts system, the Wudang sect was cradled in monasteries. Taoist priests considered kung fu as a practice, which involves a transition from activity to serenity and from serenity to activity. The alternation between activity and serenity is also concerned with a brilliant use of force and flexibility as well as *yin* and *yang* energy. This explanation acts as the underpinning principle of shadow boxing. There are many movies about the Wudang sect. Jet Li once performed aesthetically appealing Wudang kung fu in *Tai-Chi Master* (1993). Though there is still no solid evidence that Zhang Sanfeng founded shadow boxing, this school of boxing indeed bases its principles and theories on Taoist thoughts and shares much in common with Zhang's theories on martial arts. Shadow boxing exemplifies a flawless integration of

Wudang kung fu originates from Taoist thoughts. Practitioners live in deep mountains and secluded valleys to collect the energy from the natural world and strive for "oneness between man and nature."

pages 54–55

The Taoist holy place Wudang Mountain and Taoist practitioners.

at a lofty height. Assassins and martial artists live ordinary lives but would fight to death when required. The moment they reveal their weapons or skills, the mortal world turns into their *jianghu* ("river and lakes," the martial arts community). Therefore, *jianghu* acts like an extensive net, from which no one can find his way out. The movie *Reign of Assassins* (2010) depicts this inescapable dilemma. Drizzle, an assassin whose hands are covered with blood, is romantically involved with the monk Wisdom and thus decides to retreat from *jianghu*. Wisdom is the most accomplished Shaolin monk in martial arts and Buddhist meditation. He discovers that his lover is still obsessed with killing and thus is killed by Drizzle on purpose. Before his death, he tells Drizzle, "if you can lay down this sword and retreat forever, I would like to be the last person you have killed." Ever after, Drizzle lives as a recluse despite great difficulties. Martial artists have to strike a harmony between heaven, earth, and man through both physical training and spiritual cultivation in order to gain peace. They have to rise beyond the three domains in order to find a solution to trivial concerns in the mortal world.

History stands as a testimony to the belief that heaven has no mercy for man and no sense of justice. Natural disasters always coincide with turbulence in politics and disturbance in public mindset. The movie *Bodyguards and Assassins* (2009) tells about an assassination conspiracy in Hong Kong. The target was Sun Yat-Sen, the later "Father of the Nation" in the Republic of China. Those who had sacrificed their lives to protect Sun included wealthy merchants, teachers, students, opera actors, rickshaw pullers, wanderers, corrupt policemen, and a beggar who used to be rich. These characters mostly had no

martial arts, general arts, and guidance arts. It is not only useful for combat but also keep practitioners fit and helps them gain mental harmony. Practitioners can achieve the ultimate "oneness of man and nature" in a natural and peaceful way. The underpinning principles of shadow boxing maintain that man is an integral part of nature, rather than its opposition. Through millennia of evolution, Taoist thought gradually gave birth to a comprehensive sect of martial arts in Ming and Qing, thanks to the contributions of martial artists who were also Taoist practitioners.

Not every accomplished martial artist dwells in deep mountains, but all of them see themselves living a secluded life. They observe the mortal world by placing themselves idea what "revolution" meant. Everything they had done was driven by "righteousness." The corrupt policeman, played by Donnie Yen, intending to win the respect of his young daughter, confronts a group of assassins and dies heroically. The beggar, played by Leon Lai, bathes himself and puts on a decent gown, restoring his graceful bearing before he is hit by misfortune. He defies hundreds of enemies before his death, living up to a swordsman's pursuit of "spiritual purity." Sun once remarked, "In pursuit of civilized happiness, we have to first undergo civilized pains. These pains are called 'revolution.'" In the eyes of those martial artists, revolution meant nothing but sacrificing their lives for the good of later generations. Their righteous deeds in the movie should be interpreted as an elegy for their times.

Social strife escalated in Qing, finally leading to the breakout of the Taiping Rebellion (1850–1864). This disaster caused casualties approximating hundreds of millions. "Gloomy sky, dark land, and tragic life" was an accurate depiction of the late Qing society. Three martial artists in the movie *The Warlords* (2007), set during this chaotic civil war, swear to be blood brothers. In order to live, Pang Qingyun, played by Jet Li, turns into a ruthless slaughterer whose ultimate life goal is to save himself and pursue fame and wealth. Zhao Er-Hu and Jiang Wuyang do not have much choice but they still believe in the divinity and transcendence of the sworn brotherhood. The three sworn brothers drift apart but finally reunite in a dramatic way. At last, they kill each other, keeping their promises to share life and death together. *The Warlords* is adapted from a true story and reflects the failure of "righteousness" through a tragedy.

Let's go back even further. Eighteen centuries ago, back in the Three Kingdoms period, a decisive battle at Red Cliff between southern and northern forces determined the fate of hundreds of thousands of warriors.

1
2

1 In *Reign of Assassins* (2010), Drizzle is eager to live an ordinary life after changing her appearance.

2 The swordsmen in *Bodyguards and Assassins* (2009).

The northern warlord Cao Cao led his troops down to South China, while warlords Liu Bei and Sun Quan of the south, taking advantage of favorable weather and geographical conditions plus public support, joined hands and defeated Cao's army. The movie *Red Cliff* (2008) and its sequel, *Red Cliff II*, released in 2009, were adapted from the fourteenth-century novel *Romance of the Three Kingdoms*. A strategist for Liu Bei, Zhuge Liang, who had long observed nature, accurately forecasted when the southeast wind would start; South China troops were used to fighting on water and gained another advantage considering their geographical condition. Mencius, the great thinker of ancient China, used to say, "Opportunities of time vouchsafed by heaven are not equal to advantages of situation afforded by the earth, and advantages of situation afforded by the earth are not equal to the union arising from the accord of men." The interactions between general and strategist Zhou Yu, and Zhuge Liang gave birth to the ultimate battling strategies, while the brotherhood between Liu Bei, General Guan Yu and Zhang Fei also formed an unbreakable fortress. These fraternities belonged to the category of "union arising from the accord of men." Director John Woo never fails our expectations in depicting brotherhood. In his *Red Cliff,* a woman confronts the war. Zhou Yu's wife, Xiaoqiao, visits Cao in his camp late at night, hoping to appease the conflict with her femininity, cleanse a politician's ambitions with tea, and avoid war in a diplomatic way. Sometimes, inherent feminine benevolence facilitates a profound understanding of life, world, and mind. Harmony among the three realms will lead to peace. This principle is intangible to Cao, who fails to achieve harmony because of his egoism. The alliance of Sun and Liu gives Cao a crushing defeat, but at the sight of the dead soldiers and their spilled blood, who has won? Though commonly recognized as a winner in this battle, Zhou Yu admitted, "none of us is the winner," as no one had found a way to avoid the war.

As to the relationship between heaven, earth, and man, the ancient Chinese made a simple and plausible conclusion: Heaven represents *yang*, while earth stands for *yin*; man acts as a harmonizing energy for *yang* and *yin*. This harmonizing energy has a close relationship with a peaceful mind and a safe condition. Therefore, peace and safety define a superior attitude toward life and represent a common pursuit for mankind. Just as the saying goes, "the harmony between *yin* and *yang* leads to peace and safety."

1 | 2
   | 3

1 Jiang Wuyang has
no control over his
life trajectory due
to the larger social
context in the movie
The Warlords (2007).

2-3 In the movie
Red Cliff (2008),
men confront
their enemies
while women seek
solutions to avoid
war.

OF KUNG FU

Martial arts, like general arts, involve a lifelong commitment. These two types of art might converge at a certain point and lead to a transcendent wonderland. What we can do along these two endless roads is to march forward in a courageous way.

Both Chinese general arts and martial arts boast a time-honored history. One was established as a noble pursuit, while the other was solely passed down in *jianghu* ("rivers and lakes," martial arts communities); one was enshrined in official historical documents, while the other appeared only in legends.

Both men of letters and martial artists have an uncompromised passion for bamboo. Bamboo has had a place in Chinese population for millennia. In ancient China, text was written on bamboo strips with bamboo-pole brushes. These bamboo strips were later bound into books and acted as an essential medium to pass down Chinese culture from generation to generation. Bamboo is also an indispensible ingredient of the traditional Chinese lifestyle, closely associated with the Chinese like a family member. Standing in a tranquil bamboo grove, we will find ourselves a part of an emerald sea. In this sense, bamboo groves are an optimal residence for artists and also an ideal habitat for reclusive martial artists.

① Northern Shaolin Boxing
② Poking Feet and Tumbling Boxing
③ Eight Trigrams Palm
④ Snake and Crane Shadow Boxing
⑤ Intention Boxing
⑥ Yang-style Shadow Boxing
⑦ Li-style Shadow Boxing
⑧ Chen-style Shadow Boxing
⑨ Wu-style Shadow Boxing
⑩ Lost Tracking Boxing
⑪ Six Harmonies Boxing
⑫ Eight Extremities Boxing
⑬ Chopping Hanging Palm
⑭ Springing Kicks
⑮ Plum Flower Boxing
⑯ Form and Intention Boxing
⑰ Greater and Lesser Hung Kuen
⑱ Mongolian Wrestling
⑲ Kunlun Sect
⑳ Emei Sect
㉑ Qingcheng Sect
㉒ Monkey Boxing
㉓ Songxi Internal Martial Arts
㉔ Kunlun Shadow Boxing
㉕ Yingmen Boxing
㉖ Zimen Boxing
㉗ Lama School
㉘ Peacock Boxing
㉙ Reed Pipe Boxing
㉚ Great Achievement Boxing
㉛ Ghost Foot
㉜ Zhuang Fist
㉝ Wolf Soldier Combat
㉞ Li-style Boxing
㉟ Liu-style Boxing
㊱ Cai-style Boxing
㊲ Mo-style Boxing
㊳ Southern Boxing
㊴ Hung Kuen
㊵ White Eyebrow Boxing
㊶ Choy Lee Fut
㊷ Shaolin Flower Boxing
㊸ Southern Mantis Boxing
㊹ Five Plums Boxing
㊺ Stool Boxing
㊻ Natural Boxing
㊼ Martial Artists' Gathering
㊽ Feeding Crane Boxing
㊾ Hakka Wanderer Boxing
㊿ Golden Eagle Boxing
51 White Crane Boxing
52 Dragon Reverence Boxing
53 Five Ancestors Boxing
54 Wing Chun
55 Arhat Boxing
56 Dog Boxing
57 Zhang Sanfeng Style Shadow Boxing
58 Traveler Boxing
59 Qiuhe Boxing
60 Southern Boxing

61 Siming Internal Martial Arts
62 Six Harmonies School
63 Guoshu Institute
64 Through-the-back Boxing
65 Great Ancestor Boxing
66 Cannon Boxing
67 Shaolin Boxing
68 Yue-style Free Fighting
69 Shadow Boxing
70 Chang-style Boxing
71 Cha Fist
72 Hua Fist
73 Wudang Internal Martial Arts
74 Mantis Boxing
75 Sun Bin Fist
76 Boat Boxing
77 Chin Woo Athletic Association

Map of Chines

江山国术

Kung Fu

中 布 图

少北拳 ①

戳脚翻子拳 ②
八卦掌 ③
④ 蛇鹤太极
⑤ 意拳
迷宗拳 ⑩
杨氏太极 ⑥
李氏太极 ⑦ ⑫ 六合拳 ⑪
⑮ 陈氏太极 ⑧ 八极拳 潭腿 ⑭
梅花拳 吴氏太极 ⑨ 劈挂掌 ⑬

岳氏散手 ⑱
太极拳 ⑲ 螳螂拳 ⑭
长家拳 ⑳ 孙膑拳 ⑮
通臂拳 三皇炮捶 少林拳 ⑰ ㉑ 查拳 船拳 ⑯
⑭ ㉕ 华拳 ㉒
㉖ 武当内家拳 ㉓ 赵氏会 ⑰
四明内家拳 ㉑
国术馆 南拳 ㉚ 六合门 ㉒
㉓ 邱鹤拳 ㉙
白鹤拳 ㉕ ㉓ 五祖拳 罗汉拳 ㉕
自然门 ㊻ ㉒ 咏春拳 地术拳 ㉖
㊼ 武林大会 龙鹰拳 张三丰太极拳 ㉗
板凳拳 行者拳 ㉘
㊺ 五梅拳 ㊹
南派螳螂 ㊸
㊸ 少林花拳 ㊷
㊵ 白鹤门 金膺拳 ㊿
㊿ 白眉拳 蔡李佛拳 ㊶ 食鹤拳 洪拳 ㊴
㊴ 洪拳 鸣鹤拳 流民拳 ㊾
㊲ 莫家拳
㊳ 刘家拳
㊱ 蔡家拳
㊳ 南拳

江

湖

远

LASTING GLORIES
OF CHINESE
MARTIAL ARTISTS

Central Guoshu Institute

Five decades ago, in a bamboo grove by the side of the Li River, a young boy was tirelessly practicing kung fu under the guidance of his instructor, the phoenix-tailed bamboo adding a sense of holiness to the already picturesque scenery. Half a century later, the instructor has long since passed, and the once-young boy is now approaching seventy. But the moment he takes a spear in his hand, his moves are so dashing that you might question his age. With the passage of time, the phoenix-tailed bamboo has thrived. It is taken to be the incarnation of lofty and noble characters, just like the elderly martial artist, Liu Jingbang. Liu's instructor was Wang Shaozhou, known as one of the "Five Southbound Tigers" over eight decades ago.

The year 1927 witnessed the foundation of the Central Guoshu Institute (literally translated as "Central Martial Arts Academy"). The institute was under the direct leadership of the Nationalist government of the Republic of China and funded by the national treasury. It was the cradle for a number of martial artists who valued both cultural edification and martial training. Back then, the institute boasted a cluster of the most outstanding martial artists from across the country. Wang Shaozhou, who was employed by the institute at the age of thirty-six, was one of them.

Born in 1892, Wang Shaozhou was of the Hui ethnicity. He started to learn Cha fist at the age of fifteen. Cha fist was one of China's best-known boxing varieties created by the Hui ethnicity. The Cha Fist is marked with an erected and extended pose, an explosive force application, a combination of the dynamic and the static, and a balance between force and resilience. Whether

Liu Jingbang, old but vigorous, has practiced Northern Cha Fist in South China for half a century.

the practitioner is moving forward or backward, upward or downward, he has to seek a harmonized and well-coordinated state and exhibits an unrestrained, agile and tough bearing throughout the practice. In Qing, Shi Desheng, a leader of the rebels, improved and enriched Cha fist. Shi taught Cheng Shoudian his kung fu skills. Cheng, in turn, enhanced the effectiveness of its attacking and defensive moves, and then taught Wang Shaozhou the optimized version. In 1918, when serving as a commander in the army, Wang was responsible for teaching the soldiers how to wield a broadsword. He once slew four Russian enemies with a steel broadsword, applying close-quarters combat skills to battlefield fights in a flexible way. In 1928, Wang was employed as a trainer in the Central Guoshu Institute for his outstanding martial skills.

The same year, the institute designated him to disseminate martial arts in Guangdong and Guangxi with four other martial artists. The five of them were jointly remembered as the "Five Southbound Tigers." In 1932, he was invited by Li Zongren, a general leading the New Guangxi Clique, to teach boxing skills in Guilin, and was granted the rank of colonel. Serving as the chief instructor in the general headquarters of the New Guangxi Clique, he trained numerous soldiers, who later grappled with the Japanese invaders with intimidating valor on the frontier.

In 1959, an old man was struggling to push a three-wheeled cart along the street in Guilin, when two boys passing by gave him a hand. One of the two was Liu Jingbang. On their way home, Liu's friend happened to mention that the elderly man they had just helped knew a lot about martial arts. Hearing that, Liu went back to ask if the elderly man could teach him kung fu. This elderly man was actually Wang Shaozhou who had been living in seclusion for over a decade. Wang asked him to come

Along the Li River, Liu wields a traditional spear under the shade of an old tree.

to the stadium on that Saturday night. When Saturday came, Liu waited the whole night in the stadium. He was just about to leave in disappointment when Wang showed up. Wang asked if he was prepared to endure hardships. After getting an affirmative answer, Wang took Liu as his disciple. The young boy kept his word and made a lifelong commitment to practicing Chinese martial arts.

Liu was so fascinated with kung fu that he also dragged his two younger brothers and his friends to practice with him. This community of boys spent their childhoods immersed in the kung fu world. They were awe-stricken by Wang when he demonstrated his kung fu skills. The explosive power of his moves was so mindblowing that his disciples always felt it was impossible to catch up. Wang stressed practical functions, giving his disciples a competitive advantage in real combat.

After Wang's return to Guilin, Liu continued to practice kung fu under the guidance of Guo Liangzuo, who learned kung fu with Wang from the same instructor. Later, Liu found a job in a factory and served as a part-time trainer for the martial arts team he set up. In 1986, Liu founded the Good Virtue Martial Arts Association, which indicated that martial arts practitioners were supposed to be virtuous in the first place. The membership has exceeded three hundred in total. On weekends, hundreds of practitioners get together in the city stadium and practice martial arts under Liu's guidance. In the 1990s, young kung fu lovers radically decreased in number, but Liu did not give up on the remaining few, including a seven-time free-fighting championship winner. Liu cares about nothing other than martial arts and his family. He has found it greatly satisfying to have a job to support his family, a residence to take shelter in, and a bamboo grove to practice kung fu in.

Eight Extremities

The foundation of the Central Guoshu Institute heralded a thriving growth of kung fu institutes all over the country. Hebei Provincial Guoshu Institute was founded in 1928. A young student named Bao Yousheng was the most notable here. Born in 1911, Bao started to learn springing kicks at the age of eight and was recommended to study kung fu in the residence of General Xu Lanzhou at fifteen. Later, he was admitted into Hebei Provincial Guoshu Institute. While studying in the institute, Bao learned eight extremities boxing from Xu Jiafu, the then director for academic affairs. After graduation three years later, he was invited by the institute for further studies in the so-called internal-style kung fu (a practice to build up strength through breathing and other exercises of the internal organs). Later, Bao worked as an assistant tutor and served as the part-time martial arts trainer for the headquarters of the Twenty-Ninth Army of the Nationalist Party.

In his studies, Bao trained himself in muscle-bone stretching exercises, which involved unimaginable hardships. To achieve the expected results, the practitioner had to stretch his bones by manipulating his energy

circulation. For example, when practicing the move *ding hai zhen* ("pillar to pacify the sea"), the practitioner is supposed to bend down with his hands on his heels and his nose between his feet. He has to maintain this pose and circulate his energy all over the body for half an hour. After a single practice, the practitioner will find himself soaked in sweat; even the ground around his feet will be wet with his sweat. Many good martial artists will fail this exercise because it is so difficult, but Bao has endured this tough process and thus elevated himself to a higher level in terms of internal and external kung fu styles.

Bao returned to his hometown in 1949. Some young men traveled far to learn kung fu from him. In 1978, Bao was invited to stay at his disciple Wang Shiquan's residence in Beijing. Wang practiced kung fu with his instructor from dawn till sundown.

Wang has studied eight extremities boxing since 1965, but it was not until his encounter with Bao that he was exposed to the indefinite mysterious and miraculous power of martial arts. During practice, Bao would make very gentle moves but his joints and knuckles would let out cracking sounds. With the changes in movement, this sound escalated in intensity until it resembled metallic crashes. This was only achievable for those who could

2 3

1

1 Wang Shiquan, inheritor of eight extremities fist, exhibits a brilliant use of this kung fu on a square table.

2–3 Wang Shiquan practices with double hooks, and a sword.

stretch their bones through energy circulation. Bao once demonstrated the action *kao shan bei* ("against the mountain"). He faced the wall and exerted strength. The next second, the five tile-roofed rooms shook, with the glass windows snapping and dirt falling down from the ceiling. Residents in other rooms stormed out in fear of an earthquake. To achieve this, the practitioner had to exert strength against the wall thousands of times every day. It is relatively easier to lean against the wall than face the wall in practicing this action, as the latter involves a subtly brilliant use of the abdominal and the pectoral muscles. One cannot fully exploit the power of this action without years of practice. In deep autumn of 1979, Bao and his disciples had a gathering in Wang's residence, where he demonstrated the so-called *ying fan* ("eagle somersault") move, which he learned back in the Central Guoshu Institute. Bao had his nose and tiptoes pressed against the eastern wall and shrank his body. In a flash, he had already pressed himself against the Western wall before anyone present noticed. Bao always maintained that without solid internal skills and scientific methods, the practitioner can never achieve the integration of internal and external skills as well as a free control of any part of the body.

Bao passed away in 1995. Today, children in his hometown have started to practice eight extremities boxing. Thanks to his disciples' efforts, this practice has already been incorporated into schools' physical education curriculums. Wang Shiquan is a committed inheritor of the spiritual pursuit and profound meaning of his instructor and eight extremities boxing, and has won a good reputation in the Chinese martial artist community. When Wang is practicing boxing on the traditional eight immortals table (a square table seating eight people), it seems that his valorous momentum has

brought us to another world where we have the illusion that Bao is practicing in the Central Guoshu Institute. Traditional eight extremities boxing moves are evidence of Wang's identity as a practitioner of traditional kung fu, an insightful instructor and a real martial artist.

Shadow Boxing

In 1929, Beijing Guoshu Institute was founded. In the shadow boxing contest hosted by the institute, Zhang Huchen, a lean and handsome young man, claimed the Silver Shield Award. In the following year, this rising star in shadow boxing, best known for his impressive skills and sedate personality, was appointed head of Tongzhou Guoshu Institute. Later, he started to be widely recognized in the kung fu community after defeating all his challengers from various kung fu schools.

Zhang, was born in 1898. Quiet in nature, Zhang first became fascinated by martial arts in his childhood. He used to practice cannon boxing but later became attached to shadow boxing due to a chance encounter. In the spring of 1919, Zhang saw three muscular rickshaw pullers cornering a man of letters in a gown. The latter made an unexpectedly swift attack, which swept two of the three rickshaw pullers off their feet. Zhang found it really miraculous and asked the man in the gown about his kung fu skills. The latter replied that he started to learn kung fu in a local kung fu school four years ago and had just used shadow boxing to subdue his opponents. On the man's recommendation, Zhang was taken by Xu Yusheng as a disciple, and later was also instructed by Yang Shaohou and Yang Chengfu, becoming the fourth-generation

Qian Feng practices shadow boxing in a pavilion.

inheritor of the Yang-style shadow boxing. Zhang learned most of his kung fu skills from Yang Shaohou. As a quick learner and an industrious practitioner, Zhang finally became an accomplished master in this field. Zhang Huchen passed away in 1979. He taught everything he had learned to Wang Xiutian, who was the best among his six disciples and had learnt from Zhang for seventeen years.

Wang Xiutian, with a modest nature, has been practicing and diving into boxing in a low-profile manner in the past four decades. Following his instructor's instruction, he has been teaching boxing for free for decades, and has introduced the original features of shadow boxing to more people. Among Wang's disciples, Qian Feng is the most outstanding. Born in 1952, Qian

started learning kung fu since childhood. In 1986, Qian formally acknowledged Wang Xiutian as his instructor and became his first disciple. Qian was infatuated with the Yang-style shadow boxing and spent many sleepless nights trying to unveil its mysteries until he finally fully comprehended the essentials of the Yang-style small-frame shadow boxing.

According to Qian, many predecessors practicing Yang-style shadow boxing have made themselves well-known in the community all because of the unique pragmatism of shadow boxing. Actually, it may well be said that these practical combating skills make an indispensable ingredient of today's Yang-style shadow boxing. Now, Qian has made it his lifelong career and an eternal commitment to disseminate shadow boxing.

Greatly differing from other boxing varieties, the extraordinary shadow boxing tends to be ordinary in a deceiving way.

Dong Yasheng started to learn kung fu at the age of eleven. He used to be an outstanding special forces soldier and learned Shaolin boxing and Chen-style shadow boxing while serving in the army. After retiring from the army in 1984, he was often seen practicing Chen-style shadow boxing and wielding various kinds of weapons in a park in the morning. One day, an old man, claiming to have observed him for a whole month, offered to share with him a set of boxing skills. Dong was amazed by his demonstration. Dong was later informed that the elderly man was Zhao Yukun and his kung fu belonged to the variety of snake and crane shadow boxing. This variety dated back to the early Ming and was founded by Zhao Wuzhen. Zhao's great-grandson Zhao Zhenbei had elevated this set of boxing to the ultimate level. In

Dong Yasheng is skilled in various kung fu schools. His snake and crane shadow boxing is quite legendary.

order to make sure that his boxing would not be used for evil purposes, he made it a rule that for each generation, snake and crane shadow boxing could be passed down only directly from father to son. In the following six centuries, snake and crane shadow boxing maintained its original flavor. As one of the inheritors, Zhao Yukun had no offspring. He ran into Dong when seeking medical treatment in Beijing. After long and careful observation, Zhao was convinced that Dong was both skilled and virtuous. Therefore, he finally made up his mind to break the rule to teach all his skills to Dong. Shortly after he passed down all his kung fu to Dong, Zhao passed away without any regret. Different from mainstream schools, snake and crane shadow boxing was efficient in combat as the practitioner could take winding routes like a snake to restrict his opponent's movements and exert his strength in an agile but explosive way. In 2007, Dong founded the Snake and Crane Shadow Boxing Seminar in Beijing. He followed Zhao's instructions and maintained a cautious approach in the search for his inheritor.

Dong is also versed in use of flexible weapons. He is especially good at wielding nine-section whip and spear. As a policeman, Dong, taking advantage of his accomplished kung fu skill, has been dealing with homicide cases for over a decade, which is strong evidence that kung fu is also functional in other ways in modern society in addition to enhancing physical strength.

Born in 1954, Yan Guoxing started to learn the Yang-style shadow boxing from his father in his boyhood.

Yan's father was implicated in the social-political turbulence of the 1960s and 1970s. When he was back home, his miserable appearance would render his family

speechless. One time, Yan Guoxing broke the silence and asked for two yuan from his father. He made his way directly to a park to find a kung fu instructor. He was determined to learn kung fu to defend his family. After mastering the northern school kung fu, at the age of sixteen he started to learn through-the-back free-fighting skills from Yang Yongqing, who was the disciple of Gong Chengxiang, a well-known instructor in the Central Guoshu Institute. Yan was mostly interested in kung fu with an emphasis on pragmatism and efficiency. Through industrious practice, Yan finally mastered what he had learned.

In the late 1970s, Yan had already incorporated methods from various schools through rich combat experience. After returning home, he picked up shadow boxing under the instruction of his father again. Yan believed that shadow boxing skills are supposed to be

based on real combat. Since 1983, Yan has won the National Hand-Pushing Championship three times and defeated all the challengers from various countries. He is commonly recognized as the "King of Hand-Pushing."

Liu Wei was born in 1967. When he was still a boy, Liu became a victim of medical malpractice and suffered aplastic anemia. After diagnosing him, a doctor concluded he wouldn't survive to see his twentieth birthday. At fifteen, five years before Liu's death sentence, the movie *Shaolin Temple* (1982) engendered a surging interest in martial arts across the country, with more than one thousand applicants queuing up before the Dongcheng District Gymnasium to enroll in kung fu courses. Liu's family used connections to send Liu, who then was obsessed with kung fu, to a form and intention boxing class. Because of Liu's thin and weak appearance, he was

always neglected and had to practice standing exercises in a corner. Two years later, he was delighted to find that his nosebleed and gum bleeding was tapering off.

Li Bingci, the instructor of the shadow boxing class, was the fourth-generation inheritor of the Wu-style shadow boxing. Li recognized the solid foundation Liu had laid through strenuous standing exercises and started to teach Liu the Wu-style shadow boxing. Liu cherished this opportunity very much. He spent two hours practicing the Wu-style shadow boxing every day. Half a year later, Liu found himself in a better condition in terms of overall health and inner circulation. During this period, the form and intention boxing instructor who hadn't faith in Liu paired him with a training partner of a larger build, and Liu was thrown to the floor many times. Therefore, his instructor believed that he was not talented in martial arts, which had hurt Liu's pride. He vowed to the instructor

that he would defeat his opponent within three months, or else he would leave the institute. During the following three months, Liu exerted his utmost effort in practicing. Finally, he succeeded and won recognition from those who had ignored him.

With continuous shadow boxing practice, Liu not only survived his twentieth birthday but also maintained good health. The once feeble boy has now grown into an athletic adult. Liu was admitted to Beijing Sport University without taking the entry examination. After graduation, he declined the university's offer to work there as a trainer and began his career as a shadow boxing coach for nongovernmental organizations. Afterward, Liu won the national Wu-style shadow boxing championship nine successive times. Shadow boxing saved his life, and he wishes to make a contribution to shadow boxing in return.

1 | 2

1 Yan Guoxing, living by the side of the West Lake, is a well-known martial artist in pushing hands.

2 Liu Wei has an incredible connection with the Wu-style shadow boxing.

Eight Trigrams

Looking back upon the history of Chinese kung fu, we cannot miss Dong Haichuan. Dong Haichuan was the founder of eight trigrams palm, and a famed martial artist in Qing.

Dong used to travel across the country and live in an unrestrained way in his adolescent years. He had made glorious achievements in martial arts in his middle years. He later became a eunuch, some suspected because he wanted to spy on the imperial family for the rebels; others assumed that he was made a eunuch as a punishment for crimes he had committed. None of these assumptions were proven. He was thus shrouded in mystery and respected as a legend. His kung fu performance lingered in the memories of all who witnessed it. He was said to have died in peace in a sitting pose. Even his death was

intermingled with a sense of divinity.

Over the past two centuries, eight trigrams palm has been inherited and popularized, which involves contributions and commitments from generations of martial artists.

Guo Xuexin is cheerful in nature, but once he starts to practice eight trigrams palm, he seems to change into another person. His moves are marked by an integration of both force and flexibility and are ridden with killing power, leaving his opponents trembling with fear.

Born in 1951, Guo started to learn eight trigrams palm in 1964 and formally acknowledged Wang Rongtang as his instructor in 1968. Wang was an advocate for pragmatism, and his thoughts exerted a significant influence on Guo. In 1969, Guo started to work in a factory at the age of nineteen. Guo was the first generation of free-fighting athletes in Beijing and started to practice

2

1

1 Li Jinghua, skilled in actual combat, is practicing with his disciple.

2 A lethal move of Guo Xuexin.

free-fighting between 1977 and 1978. He didn't have his own gloves at the beginning and had to use repaired ones that had been discarded by the professional teams. In the early 1990s, Guo took an active role in compiling the free-fighting rules by making adjustments through actual combats. He is a witness of the birth and boom of the free fighting practice. In 1993, Guo was already an international chief referee. Now, his disciples are making impressive performances in the free-fighting arena and in eight trigrams palm contests.

Li Jinghua, also an inheritor of eight trigrams palm, share common opinions about martial arts with Guo Xuexin. Li Jinghua and Guo Xuexin find each other agreeable company. Strictly speaking, they are uncle and nephew in terms of martial arts lineage, but they prefer to recognize each other as real brothers. Born in Beijing in 1963, Li started to learn form and intention boxing from his father in childhood. At sixteen, he formally acknowledged Wang Zhongyong as his instructor and gradually grasped the essence of eight trigrams palm.

He once launched a campaign to defy showy but actually incompetent martial artists to cleanse the Chinese kung fu community. This campaign attracted a lot of attention and made quite a stir.

Form and Intention Boxing

In 1928, the Central Guoshu Institute invited Sun Lutang, a renowned master, to serve as dean of the Wudang school. Later, Sun was reallocated to Jiangsu Provincial Guoshu Institute to work as Director of Teaching Affairs. In order

Liu Shuchun is an inheritor of form and intention boxing.

to attend his lectures, martial artists would even come by boat.

Sun epitomized the northern school martial arts of the late Qing and early Republican eras. Sun was versed in a rich variety of schools and advocated for the oneness of martial arts and Taoist thoughts. His kung fu was grounded on the dichotomy of form and intention and integrated eight trigrams and shadow boxing. Sun was known as the number-one martial artist of his time.

In 1930, Sun set up a female kung fu class. His daughter Sun Jianyun, who had started to learn martial arts at seven, served as the instructor. In 1933, Sun predicted that he would pass away on November 29. His daughter immediately sent him for a physical examination in a German hospital. According to the doctor, he had no health problems. However, on November 29, Sun died in peace in a sitting pose.

Liu Shulin, a disciple of Sun Jianyun, recommended his cousin Liu Shuchun to his instructor. At lunch, Shulin carried a chair to the table and was about to sit down, when Sun stormed out from beneath the table and pushed the chair with both hands. The next moment, Shulin was thrown out of the room and flew over four or five yards before landing in the courtyard in a steady pose. Still with the chair in his hand, Shulin had maintained the trinity posture. Sun turned to Shuchun, saying, "You have to be equally steady when taking this pose; otherwise, there is no point in learning it." Shuchun was shocked and made a full commitment to form and intention boxing.

Born in 1954, Liu Shuchun has practiced form and intention boxing for four decades. In his opinion, an accomplished practitioner is supposed to imagine his opponent when practicing alone in order to perform with great ease in actual combat.

1 Di Guoyong wields
a spear in a bamboo
grove.

2 Di Guoyong
practices form and
intention boxing.

2

1

Sun Lutang used to say, "My friend Shang Yunxiang recently made an insightful observation: The integration of body and spirit will lead to nihility." Sun's words fully recognized the accomplishments of Shang.

Shang was born in 1864, and he was the disciple of Liu Cunyi and Guo Yunshen. He was short and thin in stature, less than five foot three inches in height. Despite his small build, he had established a great reputation in the martial arts community due to his impressive performance in real combat. He used to head an bodyguard agency and had successfully defeated numerous opponents. He was revered as a legend, being the founder of Shang-style form and intention boxing.

The Shang-style form and intention boxing was

passed down from generation to generation by martial artists such as Liu Huafu and Zhao Zhong. Di Guoyong is the best known among its inheritors of the fourth generation. Di, born in 1948, was troubled with arthritis in middle school, when he started to practice martial arts to improve his physical condition. In the early 1980s, Di and several other martial artists started to teach form and intention boxing at Peking University. Today, as a martial artist of eighth rank according to the Chinese martial arts rating system, Di's disciples and professional writings are widely distributed all over the world. This low-profile martial artist hopes that scientific advancements can be utilized to promote the development of traditional martial arts.

Martial Artists in Sichuan

Sichuan region is known for a number of renowned mountains, among which Mount Emei recognized as the most elegant in China and Mount Qingcheng as a Taoist holy land have added to the mystery of Sichuan kung fu. It is common to employ exaggerated description and unrealistic approach for this particular school, but what is real is that many martial artists with impressive kung fu skills are still making active performance on this land.

Songxi school of internal martial arts was created by Zhang Songxi. Wang Zhengnan, a general in late Ming, was one of the accomplished practitioners of this school. Songxi school was later disseminated to Nanjing, Sichuan, and other areas of the country, practiced and improved

on by a number of martial artists. Today, Zhao Tongqiang, a martial artist from Sichuan, demonstrated this school of kung fu to us. He explained to us that the initial pose of Songxi school was laden with a historical stance of the ancient martial artists: The fist placed on the chest stood for the determination to restore the Ming rule, while the other hand reversed on the waist implied the resolution to resist the Qing regime. Considering its connotation, this pose must have been invented by Wang Zhengnan, who was committed to overthrowing the Manchurian governance in the Qing dynasty.

Zhao Tongqiang was the twelfth-generation inheritor of Songxi school. Born in 1951, Zhao is a native of Nanchong, Sichuan Province, and has had a great affection for martial arts since childhood. In 1964, Zhao started to learn martial arts from Chen Jikang. They used to practice kung fu in a local park until the beginning of the social-

political turbulence that lasted from the 1960s to the early 1970s. When Chen was under strict governmental supervision and control, they could only practice kung fu at night.

Chen was also good at fortune-telling. He made a prophecy that Zhao would have glorious future accomplishments. He warned that Zhao should not exhibit his skills in a random way. Zhao, in his adolescence back then, was indifferent to Chen's warnings and preferred to take any challenge. At a time when martial artists tended to challenge each other without wearing any protective clothing, it was a rule that anyone who fell to the ground, shed blood, or made fewer blows would be the loser. Following this rule, Zhao found no equals in Nanchong, and thus started to travel across the country for exchanges with other martial artists. He was known for his Songxi fast boxing. In one contest, he was challenging the oldest disciple after having defeated a younger one when an elderly man appeased this fight before it got worse. Zhao was informed later that the elderly man was Lü Zijian, his opponent's instructor, who was known as the "Swordsman of the Yangtze River." Zhao admired Lü for both his skills and virtues and thus started to learn eight trigrams palm from him. Lü passed away as a legend on October 21, 2012, at the age of 119.

In 2009, as the president of the Songxi School Internal Martial Arts Association, Zhao led his team to compete in a nationwide martial arts contest in Anyang, Henan Province. The referees had never seen this school before, and even the chief referee was surprised. Later, they even paid a visit to Sichuan to research Songxi school. Today, Zhao still maintains his solemn and sedate personality and seldom smiles. We hope Zhao will popularize his Songxi school so that it could be known by the majority.

2

1

1 Zhao Tongqiang, the inheritor of Songxi internal martial arts, lives in Neijiang, Sichuan. He used to run a fight club and has made a significant contribution to the application of internal martial arts in the fighting domain.

2 Wu Chengmo from Chongqing has practiced *san yuan men quan* for four decades.

Born in 1951, Wu Chengmo started practicing boxing in 1962, focusing on *san yuan men quan* ("three element gate boxing"). His instructor is Zhongliang, a Taoist priest from Qingyang Monastery, a renowned one in Chengdu. Zhongliang was second to none on the contest arena in the Republican era. In the 1960s, Wu was admitted as a disciple of Zhongliang because of a lucky coincidence, and has finally made achievements. Wu was passionate about taking photos back then. His album showcases many photos capturing his kung fu performance. These photos capture the spiritual domain of the young martial artists in the 1970s and 1980s, as well as the kung fu customs practiced in Sichuan Province back then.

Dujiangyan City used to be known as Guan County in dynastic China. Its martial arts can be dated back to Han. In the late Qing and early Republican era, this city was known for the popularity of its martial arts. Qingcheng school martial artists value pragmatism.

Liu Suibin's grandfather and mother were graduates from Guan County Guoshu Institute. Born in North China, Liu was weak and often got sick, so he had to leave the cold region and return to his old hometown Guan County, where he began learning kung fu from his grandfather to keep fit.

Liu's instructors are all well-known. In addition to his grandfather, he also followed Qi Yuxiang, one of the "Twenty-four Swordsmen in Qingcheng," and also Song Dezhao, who was a participant in the Tai-er-zhuang Battle. Song had spent over a decade to observe Liu, and did not start to pass down all he had learnt to Liu before confirming that Liu is both talented and upright, fully reflecting the prudence of the old generation of martial artists.

Liu was also acquainted with a legendary figure named Peng Yuanzhi. Peng was one of the most outstanding graduates from Sichuan Provincial Guoshu Institute and also the arena champion in Sichuan best known for his speed and agility. Peng was one of the "Top Seven Chinese Martial Artists" that the Japanese invaders tried to win over. He served as the chief martial arts trainer for the South Sichuan Defense Force. Liu once combated with Peng. Peng changed the direction of his fist and swept Liu off his feet instead of dodging his direct attack. His single blow was so powerful that the dustpan hanging on a beam fell to the floor. Peng caught the pan before it fell to the ground and dragged Liu up, saying, "I do have something to teach you, but in other aspects, you can also enlighten me. Everyone can be both a friend and an instructor for another." These words indicate that Peng was admirable not only for his skills but also for his lofty character.

Yu Guoxiong, the chief of Qingcheng school, is also one of Liu's instructors. Yu became a Taoist priest in 1933. Three years later, Yu's instructor, who was already ninety-six years old, persuaded Yu to return to secular life. According to his instructor, Yu was obligated to join the army and drive away the Japanese invaders. At the time of parting with each other, Yu's instructor gave Yu a sword and a poem as well as a life plan: to defend the country as a soldier while young, teach kung fu at middle age, and serve as a doctor in his senior years. Leading the Broadsword Brigade of No. 140 Division, Yu wielded the sword given by his instructor and killed numerous enemies in the Tai-er-zhuang Battle. However, severely injured in the battle, Yu could not erect his back in his late years. After teaching kung fu in his middle age, Yu spent the latter half of his life on medical practice, offering the impoverished free medical treatment. He was dressed in a decent and traditional manner, always carrying a walking cane in his hand. Having lived a thrifty life, Yu donated all his wealth to the poor.

The life stories of Liu's instructors capture the turbulent history of modern China. Therefore, Liu, being the thirty-sixth-generation chief of Qingcheng school, prefers to talk more about health maintenance rather than martial arts. He must have learned from his instructors' life experiences that health and auspice are of overriding significance for everyone. Most martial artists of Qingcheng school live to age eighty. It is evident that Chinese martial arts are efficient in prolonging life.

Liu Suibin is the head of Qingcheng School.

pages 88–89

In Hongsheng Hall, President Huang Zhenjiang, the inheritor of Choy Lee Fut, is talking with Qiu Deji, the inheritor of white eyebrow boxing.

Foshan, Portal of South China Kung Fu

Guangdong had already evolved into the center of Southern School kung fu back in the Qing Dynasty. Foshan, recognized as the "Hometown of Chinese Kung Fu" was home to over one hundred kung fu institutes back then. Due to geographical adjacency to Hong Kong and Macau, many martial artists from Foshan traveled overseas for a better living condition, which had greatly promoted the popularization of Chinese kung fu.

In the Hong Sheng Hall close to the old county government of Foshan, Qiu Deji, sixty-one years old, one day came to Hong Sheng Hall, a venue for practicing Choy Lee Fut. With a long cloth-wrapped staff in hand, he strode over the threshold of the hall and took a few steps forward before retreating back. He said, "I'm a practitioner of white eyebrow fist but came to the Hongsheng Hall of Choy Lee Fut with a weapon, which is against our professional ethics. I should not break the rules." President of Hongsheng Hall, Huang Zhenjiang, welcomed Qiu, saying, "It doesn't matter! Come in!"

Qiu was born into a family of martial artists in 1951 and started to practice white eyebrow fist with his father in his childhood. He was the eighth-generation inheritor of white eyebrow fist. In the 1960s, Qiu was consigned to the countryside as an educated youth for seven years. Back then, it was common to learn kung fu in the countryside in Guangzhou Province. Once there were fights among villages, the educated youth such as Qiu also had to be part of it. Qiu is short in height and small in build but surprisingly versed in real combat. He used to score four

successive victories and could subdue his rivals with just a few moves.

Working as an electrician, Qiu has been subjected to bright light for decades and thus his vision is severely damaged. However, his weak vision has never held back his development in martial arts. Rather, it has gradually sharpened his sensitivities in other aspects. Qiu prioritizes response, speed, and force. Currently, Qiu has no disciple, and his son has moved to another city to pursue a better living, unwilling to learn kung fu from him. Qiu will be the last inheritor of white eyebrow fist in Foshan.

Back to the beginning of our story, Huang Zhenjiang, the president of Hongsheng Hall, was excited over the unexpected visit of Qiu. Qiu and Huang have known each other since childhood. They both grew up in Foshan and practiced kung fu together.

In the Republican era, the Foshan martial arts community was divided into three factions. Hongsheng Hall, known for its Choy Lee Fut, was joined by workers, traders, and farmers, with an evident communist affiliation. Zhongyi Hall, known for its Wing Chun, was mostly made up of doctors, policemen, and administrative

pages 90-91

Qiu Deji is practicing
boxing in front of
Qionghua Guild Hall.

1 | 2

1 President Huang
Zhenjiang was
selected as the
inheritor of Choy Lee
Fut.

2 He Zhuohua has
practiced Choy Lee
Fut all his life.

staff, with a close association with the Nationalist Party.
The Chin Woo Athletic Association took a neutral
stand and launched patriotic campaigns. Hongsheng
Hall reached its peak in 1921, when there were three
thousand disciples and tens of thousands of students,
largest in scale in China. Most of the disciples received
martial and medical training at the same time. As the
fourth-generation inheritor of Choy Lee Fut, Huang has
introduced kung fu to the physical education curriculums
in local primary and middle schools by teaching the
students boxing. In the autumn of 2012, he was selected as

the inheritor of Choy Lee Fut, belonging to the category of
national intangible cultural heritage.

He Zhuohua teaches Choy Lee Fut at Hongsheng
Hall. Following his father's footsteps, He Zhuohua has also
been committed to the dissemination of Choy Lee Fut all
his life. Hong Sheng Hall, with a history of over 160 years,
has a number of branches overseas. To its foreign students
distributed all over the world, the institute is their spiritual
source for learning kung fu.

Born in 1948, Chen Youmin currently serves as director of the Lion Dance Troupe of Wong Fei-hung Pavilion in Foshan Ancestral Hall. Chen started to learn kung fu in 1964 and has practiced Hung Kuen, Choy Lee Fut, and white eyebrow fist since then. In the 1970s, Chen was infatuated with lion dance and boxing and formally acknowledged Zhao Rong as his instructor. Lion dance starts with kung fu performance and climaxes with *cai ching*, in which two or more lions fight with the rival lions for a ball that represents fortune.

Lion dance performers have to observe a set of established principles. For instance, when lions from different dance troupes meet, they have to greet each other by touching each other's heads, and the performers will shake hands by stretching their arms out from the lions' mouths to display good will. For troupes that have shown

hostility and defiance, they have to fight with stylistic lion moves to see whose kung fu skills are the best.

Lion dance is culturally meaningful and technically challenging. The performers have to make brilliant use of their fingers by assigning varied tasks to each of them: Some are used to control the gears of the lion's eyes, some are used to manipulate the jaw, while others are used for some challenging moves. The performers are usually required to play for one hour in one performance, which is a test of stamina. Lion dance performers dance in different styles and belong to varied schools, while lions of different colors have a diverse array of meanings and connotations. With the aging of Chen and other top performers, people start to be increasingly concerned over the inheritance of this time-honored heritage.

2
1

1 Lingnan lion dance originates from ordinary alleyways.

2 Chen Youmin favors black lions.

2
1   3   5
    4

1 Su Yinghan is the inheritor of white crane boxing.

2-5 Su Yinghan demonstrates various defending and attacking hand gestures of white crane boxing. His finger pads bulge slightly because of years of practice.

White Crane Boxing Practitioners in Seclusion

In 1928, the first national martial arts examination was held by the Central Guoshu Institute in Nanjing. Pan Shifeng, well in his seventies, led a team from Yongchun County of Fujian to participate in the examination. His team was warmly acclaimed and heavily honored. In recognition of his team's notable achievements, Yongchun Branch of the Central Guoshu Institute was later founded, and Pan was one of its founders.

Su Yinghan was born in Yongchun County in 1945 and as a boy was fascinated by lion dance and martial arts. Being a favored disciple of Pan Ruidang, son of Pan Shifeng, Su used to travel eleven miles every day to learn white crane boxing. Later, under the instruction of Zheng Lianjia, he further improved his martial arts skills. Now half a century later, Su has become the twelfth-generation inheritor of white crane boxing and belongs to the seventh rank according to the Chinese martial arts rating system.

Impressively versed in martial arts philosophy, Su has explored the moves of white crane boxing. He can expound on the mysteries of the manual and the pithy formula of this ancient boxing for three days and nights. He also has a profound understanding of the cultural meanings of the lion dance and medical science. I once exchanged some moves with him. In a flash, he went straight for my acupuncture points, and I felt a piercing pain. When I attempted to counterattack, I felt another stabbing pain under my ribs. There was no doubt that my ribs would break if he had not spared me.

Through-the-back Boxing

Zheng Ce is another name that we cannot overlook when reading into the history of Chinese kung fu. Zhang, born in 1866, started to learn kung fu in his childhood. He had learned through-the-back boxing from various masters through chance encounters. Zhang, also versed in the Yang-style shadow boxing, incorporated through-the-back boxing with shadow boxing. Through years of practice, Zhang has achieved a high level of proficiency and was known as the "Saint of Through-the-Back Boxing."

Born in the 1960s, Zhao Yajun was the fourth generation of Zhang's disciples. Zhao, a good-mannered gentleman, had been teaching boxing in Italy for three years. He doesn't have a muscular build or a defiant look, a far cry from the stereotypical image of the martial artists in the Western mindset. Some even suspected his identity and thus came to challenge him. Zhao easily defeated his challengers, including karate masters from Germany, Italy, and other countries. He lives a quiet life and likes reading and thinking. He believes that with economic development, martial arts will evolve into an iconic spiritual pursuit in years to come.

1	3
2	

1–2 Zhao Yajun practices five elements through-the-back boxing with one of his disciples.

3 The jungle of concrete structures houses accomplished martial artists. Zhao Yajun from Langfang, Hebei, is also an inheritor of five elements through-the-back boxing.

Great Achievement Boxing

Wang Xiangzhai was born in 1885 and started to learn form and intention boxing from Guo Yunshen in 1894. Later, he created great achievement boxing, and started to set up institutes in Beijing in 1937. Li Yongzong was one of his disciples. Li Yongzong was tall, slim, and blind in one eye. Li had a lasting resentment for injustice and evil. During the Republican era, Li once saw eight hooligans armed with knives bullying a female student. He fought them barehanded. Another time, even with one eye injured, he still knocked down a number of opponents to rescue his junior fellow apprentice. Later, he was wanted by Japanese troops for having soundly beaten Japanese soldiers in Beijing. He fled to West China and served as a martial arts instructor in the Nationalist forces for one year. Anyone who has seen Li practicing exclaims that his kung fu is a flawless combination of force and beauty built on real combats, a testimony to the understanding that everything is about art in essence.

Li's disciple Xu Futong was born into a literary family in 1944. He has a great passion for traditional Chinese calligraphy, painting, and martial arts. He started with long fist, practiced boxing for years, and finally became accomplished at great achievement boxing. The first time Li Yongzong met Xu Futong, Li asked Xu, "Why do you want to learn boxing?" Xu replied, "To avoid being bullied." Li said, "Good! If you want to enhance physical strength, I will advise you to go climbing. You want to fight? I will teach you how to." Before Xu could identify the direction of Li's fists, he was beat all over and lost consciousness. When he woke up, Li asked him while drinking tea, "Are you OK? Drink some tea and you will be OK."

Xu was one of the most significant founders of the modern Chinese calligraphy in the 1985 new art movement. He believes that calligraphy is efficient in enhancing cultural edification, and traditional martial art is useful in provoking thoughts.

Xu Futong, an inheritor of great achievement boxing in Beijing, is versed in both literature and martial arts.

Wu Binlou, Creator of Beijing Feet-poking Tumbling Boxing, and His Three Disciples

Born in 1899, Wu Binlou was the creator of Beijing feet-poking tumbling boxing. He started to learn kung fu at six and became known in the martial arts community in the 1920s. Wu founded Yilin Guoshu Institute on his own in the 1930s and never stopped taking disciples and teaching kung fu. According to his diaries written after the foundation of PRC, Wu had more than a hundred disciples. He emphasized virtue education, believing that a martial artist should relieve poverty and come to the rescue of those in danger. According to Wu, modesty, prudence, and courage to deliver justice are also indispensible criteria for

a qualified martial artist. At the age of forty, Wu visited Japan as a member of the Chinese martial arts delegation. The top Japanese martial artist who was honored with a visit to the Mikado every day challenged Wu to fight. Wu, small in build and without using the kicking skill that he was particularly good at, subdued his rival with only two or three moves.

In 1950, Wu taught boxing in Jingshan Park, where his students included sons of significant Chinese politicians. In 1959, Zhang Dawei, awed by Wu Binlou's outstanding kung fu skills, formally acknowledged Wu as his instructor. In Zhang's memory, Wu always taught the disciples himself. Well in his seventies, he still demonstrated to his disciples the challenging somersault action. Back then, numerous opera performers and drama actors came to learn skills from Wu, seeking to improve their stagecraft with feet-poking tumbling boxing. Wu was a clean man. Whenever he took a blanket on his bike, his disciples would know that they would practice ground tumbling that day.

After Wu's death, Zhang switched to studies of martial arts history and has made a great effort to promote the Wu-style kung fu. He is conversant with ancient and modern learning. Whenever he talks about the developmental trajectory of Chinese martial arts, he impresses others as "a walking encyclopedia."

Hong Zhitian, Zhang Dawei's junior fellow apprentice, was born in Beijing in 1946. He was instructed by the Manchurian martial official He Shouyan, who was accomplished at both medical science and martial arts and worked as an orthopedist in a hospital. Through training by Dr. He, Hong laid a solid foundation in both medical and martial domains. Later, Hong heard that Wu Binlou was an outstanding martial artist. Therefore, he visited Wu every day and did housework for him for half a year until Wu was willing to take him as his disciple.

According to Wu, Hong was "easy to train but difficult to discipline." He was easy to train because he was industrious, talented, and good at making associations in comprehending something. He was difficult to discipline because he was also a troublemaker who was fierce in nature and always challenged people to fight. Therefore, Wu asked Hong to leave three times. But cherishing his talent, Wu finally called him back, instructed him all by

himself, and taught him everything he had learned. After Wu's death, Hong totally occupied himself with martial arts philosophies and committed himself to documenting ancient boxing manuals passed down to him. In order to study anatomy, Hong took regular courses in medical schools twice and noted his own observations of combat and kung fu exercises. His disciples at home and abroad exceed fifty in total.

Born in 1950, Zhong Haiming was still young when Zhang Dawei and Hong Zhitian were already experienced practitioners of feet-poking tumbling boxing. Zhong recalled, "Back then, it was a great honor for me to carry the broadswords for those senior disciples."

In the summer of 1963, his parents took him to Jingshan Park to visit Wu Binlou. Wu was already sixty-five, but he could do a dozen somersaults in a row. Lying on the ground, he could throw himself into the air simply

2 3
1   4

1,4 Renowned martial artist Wu Binlou was one of the most important inheritors of feet-poking tumbling boxing in Beijing. He practices with a tobacco pipe, a particular weapon in this boxing variety.

2 The seal of the Yilin Guoshu Association.

3 Wu's ring can be used as a seal.

1

2

1 Zhang Dawei is wielding a tobacco pipe in his own courtyard.

2 Hong Zhitian is holding a broadsword once belonging to the imperial guard in Qing dynasty.

page 106–107

Zhong Haiming, with a long vision, is performing kung fu on the roof of a 249.9-meter tower. Behind him are iconic buildings of Beijing.

by patting on the ground. Zhong was awestruck and decided to learn kung fu from Wu at once. In the early 1970s, Zhong was imprisoned in a tent at below freezing temperatures for over three months as a victim of political persecution and suffered from severe amyotrophy in his left leg. However, he survived the harsh conditions by giving himself acupuncture with a six-inch silver needle he brought with him. After recovery by practicing kung fu, he escaped from three traffic accidents and two construction collapses, which demonstrates his agility.

Zhong graduated from Beijing University of Posts and Telecommunications with a master degree in engineering. In 1982, he finished the translation of *Bruce Lee's Fighting Methods* and thus was the first person to introduce Lee's Jeet Kune Do to mainland China.

Having studied and practiced kung fu for fifty years and survived much turbulence and hardship, Zhong founded the Martial and Medical Institute. The courses are martial arts, medical science, health maintenance, acupuncture, calligraphy, painting, traditional Chinese opera, and others. Visiting professors include Zhu Heting, Xu Futong, Wu Bin, Zhang Dawei, Shi Deyang, and Zhu Naizheng. He has always remembered what are the most important elements of martial arts: skill, art, and medical science, just as his instructor Wu Binlou believed.

Endless Pursuit of Martial Arts and Its Tao

Born in 1937, Wu Bin migrated to Shanghai shortly before the breakout of the Battle of Shanghai and the subsequent loss of Shanghai to Japan. Wu still has a vivid memory of this city in the Anti-Japanese War years, when, to Wu, it was defined by the conflict between the bustling city and inadequate supplies, gloomy wars and a carefree childhood, an uptight life and a heartwarming family, and energetic youth and a complicated political climate. Everything seemed to be ridden with conflicts.

Due to his talent in sports, Wu joined the Chin Woo Athletic Association in middle school and applied for the Central Institute of Physical Education (today's Beijing Sport University) in 1958. After graduation, Wu Bin started to work as a martial arts trainer in Beijing Shichahai Sports School. Three of Wu's fellows were from the former Central Guoshu Institute in the Republican era. One of them was already in his nineties but could still do the splits. Wu took every opportunity to learn from them. Besides these trainers, Wu also traveled across the country to visit renowned instructors and incorporate the strengths of various schools into his own kung fu. Back then, a number of martial artists lived low-profile lives and declined to expose their real identities to others. Wu once ran into a young girl who specialized in feet-poking tumbling boxing. She simply stomped on a pile of three bricks, and all three bricks broke in half, which was breathtaking.

In the turbulent years of social-political movements in the 1960s and 1970s, it was a national policy to discourage kung fu practice. During that special period, the faculty was prohibited from teaching combat techniques and was required to focus instead on actions and poses. In this way, Chinese martial arts gradually transformed into a form of body-building exercises and entertainment, and martial arts schools were closed down. Despite this political climate, Wu continued with his practice and organized many activities to enhance exchanges among various martial artists. Later with the help of other martial artists, Wu founded the Beijing Martial Arts Team and served as the chief coach. In training, he always reminded athletes that all the martial arts routines they were learning encapsulated the real combat experience of accomplished martial artists of previous generations. The Beijing Martial Arts Team was a great attraction for young boys in Beijing. In 1979, the First Martial Arts Performance Contest was held in Nanning,

1 | 3
2 |

1–3 Wu Bin
practices boxing at
Zhong Haiming's
Martial and Medical
Institute.

---
page 112–113

Zhu Heting, already
in his eighties,
is energetic and
firm. He is known
for his impressive
contribution to both
martial arts and
medical science.

竹林深

YOUNG
COMMITTED
MARTIAL
ARTISTS

Wing Chun Practitioners

Wang Zhipeng was born in 1976 on the prairie of Inner Mongolia. He started to travel around the country to visit renowned instructors at an early age and learned Shaolin boxing, free fighting, Tae Kwon Do, great achievement boxing, and other real combat kung fu. In the 1990s, Huang Chunliang, an accomplished Wing Chun practitioner and disciple of Ip Man, launched a Wing Chun training project in Beijing. Wang Zhipeng attended the class out of love and passion for Wing Chun, and joined Huang to popularize this school of Chinese kung fu.

Wang makes full use of his physical strength to optimize his kung fu skills. The year before last, I exchanged some moves with him, and his arms felt as firm as timber. Last year, I tried some hand moves with him, and found that he had mixed both softness and toughness together to maximize the power of his strikes. This year, I lost my balance when I was trying to block his move.

His disciples are distributed across the country. He frequently appears on various media and has become a kung fu star in the Chinese public opinion.

Caius Nesvadba is a former British Tae Kwon Do champion. When taking Wing Chun classes at the University of Oxford, he was awestruck by the explosive

Wang Zhipeng, in the prime of his life, is one of the most important Wing Chun instructors in Beijing.

power of Wang Zhipeng's moves and fell in love with Chinese kung fu instantly. He formally acknowledged Wang as his instructor and spent several months in Beijing learning kung fu from Wang. Seven years have passed, and Nesvadba is now an influential Wing Chun instructor in the UK. Ninety percent of kung fu practitioners practice in parks, transforming parks into an integral part of *jianghu*. Nesvadba once challenged a local Wing Chun instructor in a British park and won.

Ding Sukai is a young artist. He started to learn Wing Chun in 2012. Kung fu practice has brought changes to his personality. Ding, who used to be quiet in nature, has turned into a sports person. He drives with his boxing gloves in the car and also installs a wooden dummy in his studio. Believing kung fu will be a lifelong pursuit for him, Ding spends all his free time practicing Wing Chun.

Curator Song Jirui is Ding Sukai's junior fellow apprentice. He cannot attend class due to a busy working schedule. Therefore, Ding teaches Song all he has learnt from class. Being a father-to-be, Song hopes his own child will practice Wing Chun in future.

Wang Zixuan was born in Liaoning. Her entrance into the kung fu world was quite dramatic. When she was seven years old, Wang's mother took her to enroll in a dance class taught by a renowned dancer. The enrolling site was so crowded that Wang was about to return home with her mother when they came across a room filled with young kung fu practitioners. An instructor of senior age observed Wang's body proportion and told Wang's mother that Wang would excel at kung fu and that he would like to teach Wang for free. With her mother's consent, Wang started to practice kung fu. Due to her outstanding talent, she is now a professional kung fu practitioner. Wang was admitted to the Central Academy of Drama in Beijing and started to get involved in movies and TV dramas. In 2009, Wang was introduced to Beijing Wing Chun Association as a member of the movie crew and thus started to practice this southern school kung fu.

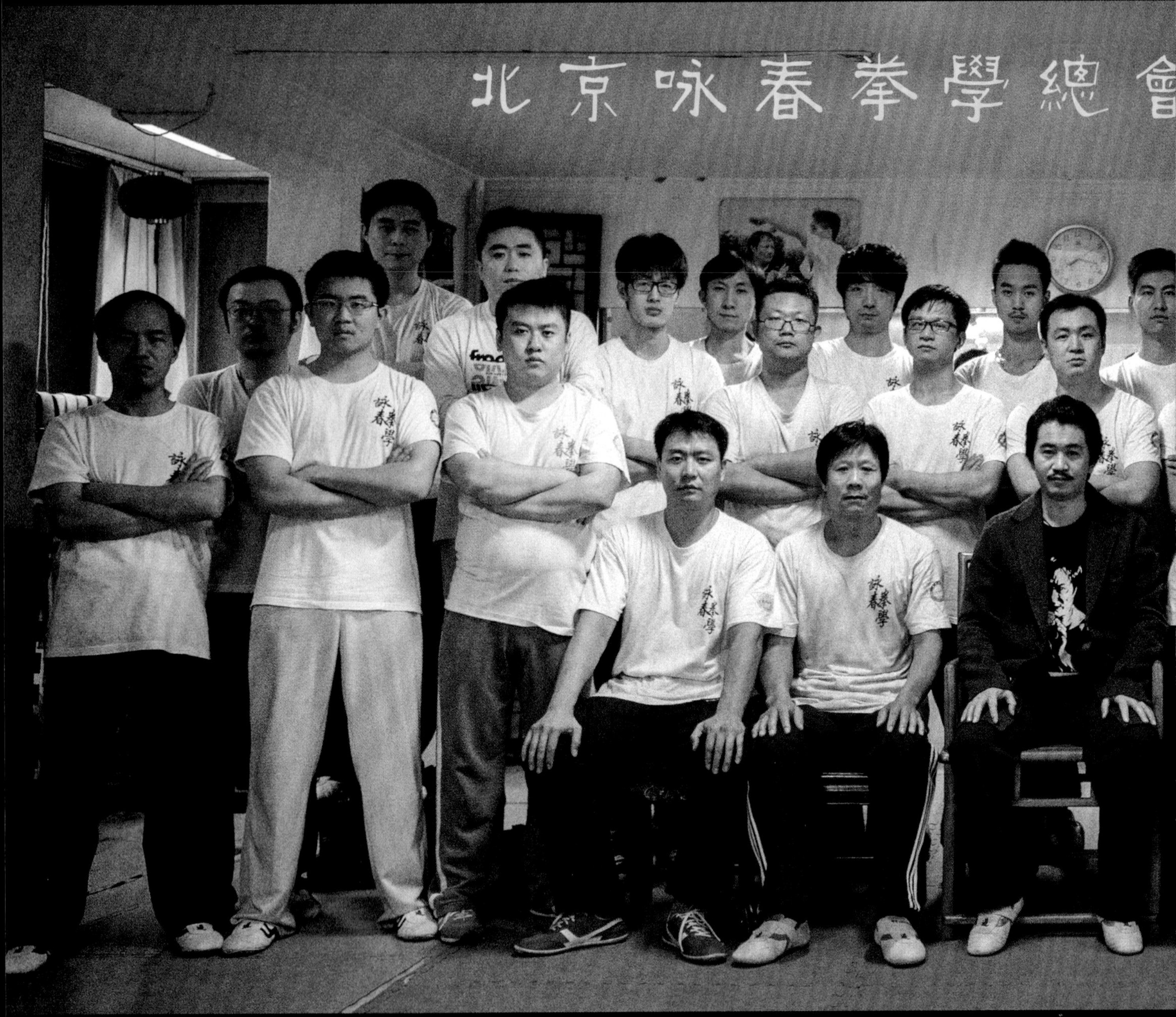
北京咏春拳學總會

合影留念 公元二零一二年十二月

Wudang and Shaolin Kung Fu Practitioners

Hu Pengfei, with Sishan being his Taoist name, was born in 1987. He started to learn external martial arts at twelve and later switched to the Wudang kung fu. He was the sixteenth-generation disciple of the Sanfeng sect of the Wudang school and the inheritor of internal martial arts.

Highly talented, Sishan is accomplished at internal martial arts, Taoist kung fu, and Taoist health maintenance practice. He started to work as an independent instructor at seventeen and traveled around the country to visit renowned masters. On his way, he was admitted to the Dragon sect of the Quanzhen school and was later selected as the youngest resident priest in the temple. He has fully grasped the *yin-yang* religious rites in a systematic way.

Recognized as the "Master of Great Achievements," he is often dispatched to local Taoist temples to conduct Taoist rituals.

Sishan is still a young man. He knows how to surf the Internet, and often utilizes his blog to popularize Taoist theories. He is such a skilled driver that driving on zigzagging hilly roads is a piece of cake for him. In martial arts, he has maintained a great passion for free fighting and Tae Kwon Do. Some younger priests want to become his disciples, but Sishan replied, "We are of similar age and should be brothers. If I acknowledge you as my disciple, you wouldn't like to play with me like a friend anymore."

A sense of uncomplicated innocence can be seen in his eyes. In many ways, he is still the young kung fu practitioner named Hu Pengfei. His unrestrained nature, quick wit, carefree lifestyle, and easygoing personality are all exemplifications of his indifference to competition and aloofness from materialistic pursuits.

1 Hu Pengfei demonstrates anti-evil hand gestures in Taoism.

2–3 Hu Pengfei practices kung fu in a Taoist temple.

1-3 Shi Deyang performs Shaolin boxing by Red Maple Lake in Guiyang, Guizhou.

Born in 1965, Shi Deyang is the thirty-first-generation martial arts inheritor of Shaolin Temple and has practiced Shaolin kung fu for more than three decades. He endured numerous hardships and survived countless injuries before becoming an accomplished practitioner. He used to serve as the chief coach of all the Shaolin martial monks and is skilled in arhat boxing, iron palm, cudgel play, sword and other varieties of kung fu. Every move of his kung fu is marked with a traditional and classic flavor. He can also fully display the explosive force of Shaolin kung fu which can be used to discipline the rival in a flash within a limited area.

Young Practitioners and Instructors

In the Republican era, Quanzhou Guoshu Institute was committed to popularizing five ancestors boxing and had trained a lot of disciples.

Born in 1972, Zhang Xiaofeng has developed a great passion for martial arts since childhood. At fourteen, he followed his father to learn boxing from Su Zaifu, an instructor of five ancestors boxing. In the Shanwaishan Guoshu Institute established by Zhang, cudgels of various lengths are suspended vertically to ensure straightness. With a cudgel in hand, Zhang can wield it with the vigor of a tiger. When performing five ancestors boxing, he is fierce and dashing in every movement. Using distinctive breathing methods, he has exemplified an intimidating valor. Zhang is versed in a rich variety of kung fu styles, among which he is especially good at using walking-stick cudgels and paired broadswords.

Zhang is the sixth-generation inheritor of five ancestors boxing. Thanks to his effort, Southern Shaolin five ancestors boxing in the form of bodybuilding exercises has been disseminated in local elementary schools, which will help train new generations practicing this traditional boxing.

Bao Ligao was born on the prairie of Inner Mongolia. Born in 1980, he started to practice wrestling at twelve and learn free fighting at fourteen. Free fighting is a competitive sport that integrates various traditional Chinese kung fu schools. Bao has won world championships in free fighting and free boxing contests many times.

Recently, Bao has played heroic characters in movies and TV series and is committed to promoting Chinese free-fighting contests.

1
| 2 3 4

1 Zhang Xiaofeng is the inheritor of five ancestors boxing in Quanzhou, Fujian.

2 It takes more than twenty days to make a cane shield.

3 Handy farming tools can also be used to practice kung fu.

4 Southern cudgels need to be vertically suspended.

Wang Shuangzhong learned boxing from his father in his childhood. As an adult, he practices free fighting, Tae Kwon Do, and eight trigrams fist. He has successfully promoted Tae Kwon Do among Shanghai universities and thus has made some inspiring conclusions concerning the management and operational approaches of martial arts. Wang hopes to reorganize the boxing routines and optimize the techniques on the basis of the five-element theory, the *yin-yang* theory, and modern technologies so that all beginners can have a quick start and Chinese martial arts will be disseminated to each corner of the world. In order to achieve this objective, he has conducted extensive research on martial arts theories. His work presents some fresh thoughts and unique ideas. In recent years, Wang has traveled between China and the United States to promote Top Win Do, a dissemination mode for martial arts.

Zhang Qinglian, the third-generation inheritor of the Yin-style eight trigrams palm, used to serve as a coach in Beijing Guoshu Institute. He once participated in the Nanjing Martial Arts Arena Contest and won third place. Xu Shixi learned from Zhang Qinglian and later also visited other renowned instructors. He has contested with outstanding kung fu practitioners from across the country and has never been defeated. He is a rising star in the kung fu arena and arrests more and more attention in recent years.

Captain Hao Bowen, born in the 1980s, learned the Yin-style eight trigrams palm and Chen-style shadow boxing from Xu Shixi. Stepping on his boarding bag, this

1	2
	3

1 Bao Ligao is a world champion in free fighting.

2 Wang Shuangzhong, the creator of Top Win Do.

3 Eight trigrams boxing manual written by Wu Lianzhi, and a hand gesture to throw a dart.

young pilot said, "kung fu is learned from practice instead of observation."

Zhao Fengyong, a practitioner of the Yin-style eight trigrams palm, was instructed by Zhu Baozhen. He started to learn kung fu since an early age, and has studied long fist, Shaolin boxing and later internal martial arts. His moves of eight trigrams palm are forceful and aesthetic, and his eight trigrams spear moves are smooth and are of endless changes. According to Zhao, kung fu practitioners should not only rely on instructions but also depend on themselves to think about and dig into the essence of kung fu by valuing real combats and routines at the same

time, as the latter is actually ridden with rich meaning. Among his disciples, the Chinese ones are relatively reserved in nature, and often stop their move right after touching the opponent in combats, but the Western ones are straightforward in nature, and would spare no effort in attacking. It is difficult to tell which approach is better. Everyone can be accomplished through hard work.

Liu Dali was born in Taiwan, in 1984 and started to learn Hung Kuen at seven.
In 1932, Xiang Haiqian, one of the best-known leaders in to the Revolution of 1911, founded the Wu Sheng Shan branch of Hongmen in Shanghai. Liu

Huijin, Liu Dali's father, is president of Wu Sheng Shan. The following three centuries have witnessed historic transformations. The undertaking to overthrow the Qing and restore the Ming has already been irrelevant to our times, and Hongmen has also undergone transformations in thought. Hongmen aims for legitimacy, public good, and innovation. Its adherents are also documenting and researching the ritual culture of Hongmen and will apply for an inscription into the List of World Cultural Heritage.

Liu began participating in international martial arts contests in his sophomore year and is now completing his master's degree at Beijing Sport University. The theme of his graduation thesis will be Hongmen kung fu. Liu is

devoted to the inheritance and development of Chinese martial arts. He hopes to popularize Hung Kuen and make his own contribution to transform Chinese kung fu into an international culture.

The girl who confronts herself in the mirror in the photo below is named Xiang Yuhe. She started to learn kung fu at six. Her parents hope that she will enhance her willpower through practicing kung fu so that she will never lose courage no matter what difficulties she might encounter in the future. Xiang is a kung fu lover. She says she will not stop practicing at least until college.

1 | 2

1 Hao Bowen, a pilot, practices the Yin-style eight trigrams palm.

2 Zhao Fengyong is the inheritor of the Yin-style eight trigrams palm.

Natural Boxing Practitioners

Natural boxing, shrouded in mystery, is known for the scarcity of its practitioners and its legends of swordsmen and assassins. Its inheritance trajectory was discontinued through generations. Therefore, it is impossible to identify its origin. Natural boxing stays out of the martial arts community. Its followers never identify themselves openly.

One of the best known of its adherents is Du Xinwu, who used to serve as the bodyguard of Sun Yat-Sen and was known as the "Supreme Swordsman." Another renowned follower was Wan Laisheng. Chen Shaoqiang, the fifth-generation disciple of natural boxing, was born in the late 1960s. He was instructed by Lin Zhiqian, a disciple

to Wan Laisheng. As an armed policeman, he once won the championship in an army contest. According to him, your signature move should be the one you are most skilled in.

Natural boxing practitioners are not common in North China. One of them is Liang Zhili, a policeman. Born in 1967, Liang started to learn kung fu from Chen Jicai in 1983, but Chen never told him which school he was practicing. Liang was informed that he was practicing natural boxing until Chen formally acknowledged him as a disciple nine years later. In 2007, he was selected as the first disciple of Chen. A century has passed since Chen's instructor started practicing natural boxing. This century must have witnessed millions of incidents and anecdotes

that have since been forgotten.

Liang's moves differ little from those of Chen Shaoqiang, though they are living in North and South China respectively. Take a close look, you will find that the shapes of their mouths are identical when taking breath during kung fu practice.

Yang Sheng is also a practitioner of natural boxing. Yang started to learn from Wan Laisheng at eight and is highly skilled in this genre.

Yang joined the army in his youth and used to work as a trainer in the special forces. He has a unique understanding of traditional kung fu and modern combat techniques. In recent years, he has fully committed himself to training close-range bodyguards, which involves the establishment of a unique guarding system on the basis of traditional kung fu. Yang can enable ordinary athletes to master real combat techniques within a week, because he is good at optimizing the distinctive physical resources of independent athletes by making best use of their physical strength. According to Yang, angular corners of a book, baseball bats, and other objects can be transformed into lethal weapons if you want to. Yang has invented a flexible whip, a new soft weapon that blends the traditional flexible whip and short cudgel with badminton techniques, a highly powerful and inconspicuous weapon.

Natural boxing, enveloped in mystery, used to be the cradle of the most outstanding assassins, but interestingly, today's natural boxing produces armed policeman instead, and Yang is committed to training bodyguards whose responsibility it is to guard against assassins.

1

2

1 Yang Sheng, a practitioner of natural boxing in Xiamen, practices with a distinctive personal weapon.

2 Liang Zhili is a practitioner of natural boxing at Langfang, Hebei.

Marco Polo in Today's Boxing Community

Byron Jacobs has been to Cyprus, South Africa, Brazil, and the United States. The frequent changes in his living environments explain his strong tolerance. He came to China to learn form and intention boxing from Di Guoyong.

Jacobs was born in 1980, and he started to learn karate and judo at five. Later, he fell in love with Chinese kung fu, and his instructor was Yang Lihua, then a trainer in South Africa's National Martial Arts Team and now his wife. Byron has grown from a martial athlete into an international martial arts referee. He has witnessed Chinese martial arts' bidding process to become an event in the Olympic Games. He has experienced the changes in the scoring system in martial arts contests and has participated in the tour performance aiming to promote Chinese martial arts in South Africa.

As a referee, Byron believes that routine contests are not the same with traditional martial arts, though the routines originate from traditional martial arts.

Modern Swordsman

Zhang Hai started to learn kung fu at thirteen and is passionate about reproduction of ancient weapons and versed in weighing and producing broadswords and swords. He used to work as the weapon and combat consultant for *Detective Dee and the Mystery of the Phantom Flame* (2010) and *The Lost Bladesman* (2011). He hopes to score accomplishments in action movies in the future.

1 | 2

1 Byron Jacobs has cupped his hands to pay respect, which manifests his wish to befriend other martial artists and contruct a martial arts community.

2 Zhang Hai and his tang knife with an extremely sharp edge.

A Woman's Martial Arts Villa

It is very difficult to visit Zou Fan, as the road leading to her martial arts villa is very challenging, but upon arrival, you feel greatly relieved. It is the same with kung fu practicing: The process is painstaking, but the result will be rewarding.

Zou, born in 1965 in Chongqing, used to learn from renowned instructors and compete in the arena. Now, she has chosen to live in deep mountains and invest every penny she has to construct roads and the martial arts villa, which she hopes to serve as an exchange arena for martial artists. Nowadays, the villa has taken shape, and her disciples are practicing with her in the green mountains.

Zou Fan has five instructors. Wang Youfu, a combat master who taught Zou in her childhood, has given her a solid foundation. Zou has practiced Kunlun boxing, Minshan boxing, Shaolin boxing, great achievement boxing, shadow boxing, Meihua boxing and Hung Kuen, etc. She began to learn Kunlun shadow boxing from Duan Zhiming in 1974. Zou spent six years learning and finally mastering Kunlun shadow boxing. After five generations' inheritance, today Kunlun shadow boxing has only three practitioners, including Zou Fan. Among the three, one has quit; one has not taken disciples; only Zou is committed to the popularization and inheritance of this boxing.

According to Zou, man's soul grows in interaction with nature in deep mountains. By simply sitting still and being lost in meditation, we can achieve spiritual release.

1 | 2

1 Zou Fan practices Kunlun shadow boxing in thick fog on Luolai Mountain, which has an altitude of more than 3,200 feet.

2 Zou Fan's disciples practice kung fu in the martial arts villa.

Chin Woo Heroes

Foshan Chin Woo Athletic Association was founded in 1921, nearly a century ago. Today's Foshan residents, with a rich heritage for martial arts, are still living up to the Chin Woo spirit which highlights the importance of enhancing physical strength to protect the country.

Eagle claw boxing belongs to Northern Shaolin boxing, also known as eagle-claw tumbling boxing. Liu Fameng used to be the trainer of the Eagle Claw sect at the Foshan Chin Woo Athletic Association. His disciple Zeng Kun passed down his kung fu to Du Rui. In 2004, a kung fu practitioner who had learned boxing in North China went back to Foshan to challenge all the martial arts schools. He invited TV station employees to tape his contest with Du Rui at the Chin Woo Athletic Association. At first, he performed hard *qigong* and displayed his disregard for his rivals. At the very beginning of the contest, Du used springing kicks to attack him. When he attempted counterstrike, Du utilized eagle claw boxing to attack his acupuncture points and elbow his crucial parts, throwing his rival to the wall. All the mirrors were shattered at the blow, and his rival was defeated. Du Rui has become known for his kung fu. The challenger defeated by Du Rui might have no idea that Du, quiet in nature, is actually a professional architect.

Born in 1963, Zhang Songqing was the seventh-generation inheritor of Southern Shaolin boxing. Currently, he works as the deputy president of the Foshan Chin Woo Athletic Association.

Zhang started to learn kung fu at thirteen out of interest. Many outstanding martial artists spent their whole life visiting kung fu masters, aiming to be skilled at more boxing varieties. Highly loyal, Zhang felt that learning other boxing varieties would be a betrayal and thus has focused on Southern Shaolin boxing all his life. However, he has made a comprehensive use of this boxing and finds it enough.

In his adolescent years, he accompanied his elder brother to Guangzhou to run some errands and was knocked down when crossing the road. The troublemakers who had knocked him down called their gang to bully him, but Zhang threw one of the bullies to the other side of the road with a single blow. Awestruck by his kung fu skills, no one dared to come forward. Later, his instructor required that he no longer compete or fight with others. Zhang had kept his promise.

Zhang is now living a simple and carefree life. He is never concerned over the current development of Chinese martial arts. He believes that as long as the routines are existent, the art can be inherited in a continuous way.

Tianhai Restaurant dates back to 110 years ago. It is the get-together venue for various schools in Foshan. Even some waiters and waitresses here are accomplished kung fu practitioners. Zhang Songqing invited us for dinner here and introduced me to a legendary Hung Kuen instructor named Wu Deming.

Wu used to serve as an instructor in the People's Armed Police, and he began to practice Hung Kuen after retirement from the army. Now, he serves as the deputy president of Foshan Chin Woo Athletic Association.

In the spring of 2007, Wu was instructing his disciples to practice kung fu in a park when he saw three men wielding knives chasing after a security guard

1
2

1 Du Rui performs some signature moves of eagle claw boxing.

2 Zhang Songqing is practicing Southern Shaolin boxing on a long table. Behind him is the portrait of Huo Yuanjia, the emblem of the Chin Woo Athletic Association, as well as an inscription by Sun Yat-Sen, literally translated as "The determination to promote martial arts."

covered with blood. Wu subdued the three gangsters with effective kicking skills. This gang had committed dozens of robberies and was so bold that they had initiated an attack on the patrol force nearby. The security guard who was being chased remembered that there was a place where people often practiced kung fu and thus ran here for help. Later, under the assistance of the Chin Woo Athletic Association, the local police successfully arrested these robbers.

The phonation exercises of Foshan Hung Kuen are already extinct. When doing the tiger-claw hand and the crane-beak hand, practitioners were supposed to produce different sounds. However, in the turbulent years of the social-political movements of the 1960s and 1970s, people had to practice in secret, not daring to make any sound. Therefore, the phonation exercises fell out of usage. Wu is now committed to documenting this school of kung fu.

Kung Fu Kid

Ye Yuanxin, the fifth-generation inheritor of Wong Fei-hung, spends her life either studying at school or practicing kung fu. Sometimes, she also participates in kung fu performances. Ye was born in 2002. She started to learn kung fu at four, performed kung fu at five, and participated in various kung fu contests at eight. When Ye was nine years old, she auditioned for the part of Ip Man's disciple in *The Grand Master*.

The shy little girl never performs kung fu in front of her classmates. Brought up in a kung fu family in Foshan, which has an established martial arts tradition, Ye will definitely continue to practice.

The martial artists discussed in this chapter belong to different age groups and are accomplished at martial arts to different extents. Some practice kung fu for a living, while others are driven by interest. Some have not reached their climax, while others are in the prime of their careers. They are just a small part of the Chinese martial arts community, but have encapsulated the look of a typical Chinese martial artist. They perform on stools, tables, boarding bags, and bridges, make somersaults in the air, look at themselves in a mirror, take in the view on top of a tower, or stomp on rocks. The distance between them and the ground is that gap between their kung fu skills and their kung fu dreams.

1 2
3

1 Wu Deming practices with a pair of broadswords in his Virtue-building Martial Arts Club.

2 Instructor Wu practices Hung Kuen on a long stool. The wall is covered with the banners and medals he has won.

3 Ye Yuanxin, dressed in black, jumps onto the wall of an elementary school corridor and practices Hung Kuen passed down through her family.

CHAPTTR III
LEGACY OF KUNG FU

Once I met a young boy who would put down his schoolbag and start doing leg-pressing and standing exercises the moment he got back to his impoverished family from school. Sweat was rolling down his cheeks but he was never distracted. His father was trained in kung fu by his grandfather and was training him in the same way. The tough training had made it easier for the boy to endure hardships in life. Hearing his story, I wondered whether he would still engage himself in intensive training when he grew up, when he has to worry about being admitted into a famed university, getting a decent job, marrying the girl he loves, paying the mortgage, and supporting his parents. In these cases, would he still continue with the training? What about his son? Would he practice kung fu in an equally industrious way? What about his grandson? What will the Chinese martial arts have evolved into by then?

Bamboo needs an adequate supply of water, earth, and sunshine in order to grow. Today, we are overwhelmed by flowers, while bamboo has gradually become a rarity. Fortunately, bamboo can endure freezing cold and other harsh conditions. Once it gains maturity, it will not yield to any hardship. I hope this metaphor will also apply to later generations of martial artists.

浪
淘
沙

EVOLUTION
OF CHINESE
KUNG FU

Chinese martial arts are largely based on *The Book of Changes* and various thoughts from the pre-Qin times. *The Book of Changes* acts as the origin of natural philosophy and ethic practice in traditional Chinese thoughts. The theory that holds that the five elements reinforce and restrain each other at the same time defies the idea of there being a number one martial artist in the world. Instead, it maintains that no martial artist is the best, because there is always someone better in another aspect. Everything is relative. This belief shares great similarities with the theory of relativity as proposed by Albert Einstein thousands of years later.

Under the influence of the Confucian "benevolence" thoughts, a martial artist is expected to be of noble character. He is supposed to show his opponent due respect, oppose using destructive moves, and remain polite and modest after achieving success. All these expectations have become fundamental for martial arts practitioners in later generations. Mencius once remarked, "The superior man nerves himself to ceaseless activity," which encourages and inspires the practitioners in an enduring way.

The "Weak and Strong Points" theory in *The Art of War* has exerted a profound influence on martial arts

theories. This theory has two meanings. First, one should appear to be weak so that his rival cannot identify his strength and skills; and second, one should utilize his strong points to attack his rival's weakness, which requires observing and understanding his opponent in the first place. Just as the Chinese saying goes, "If you know your enemies and know yourself, you can win a hundred battles without a single loss."

Laozi believed in "conquering the unyielding with the yielding" and "overcoming the strong with the weak," which is the defining characteristic of Chinese martial arts. Through kung fu training, the weak can subdue the strong; the female can defeat the male, while the elderly can bring the youthful to surrender. According to *Tao Te Ching*, "Man follows the way of earth, earth follows the way of heaven, heaven follows the way of Tao, and Tao follows its own nature." Each and every kung fu practitioner has to start with the standing exercises, which are believed to be fundamental and exemplary of the "man follows the way of earth" theory. We have to learn from the plants that take root, gain power from the land, and transfer that energy from the root and express it aboveground in an explosive manner.

For millennia, with the gradual development of Chinese philosophy, numerous martial artists have contributed their own experiences and understandings, which led to the further evolution of martial arts. In ancient China, disciples always started by focusing on their shapes and energy. During basic training, the instructors would observe their virtues and talents. When the disciples did well in the standing and breathing exercises, instructors would make a distinction between them: Those virtuous but of inadequate talent would learn combat skills so that they would work as residence guards,

This eight trigrams illustration depicts the four directions and their representations in ancient China, tortoise in the north, rosefinch in the south, tiger in the west and dragon in the east.

bodyguards, or constables; those with impressive talent and morality would be trusted with boxing skills effective in killing. Later, these disciples had to learn how to conceal their skills to fit in with ordinary people. Chinese martial artists have to practice all their lives. Martial art is about endless physical and mental pursuits, which differs significantly from modern sports aimed at competitions that value accelerated training. One can seldom become an outstanding martial artist overnight.

The birth of showy but impractical kung fu was inevitable. We can imagine that many martial artists had to make a living by working as entertainers. In addition, kung fu performance was also an indispensable ingredient of festivals and galas. True kung fu might be intangible to a lay audience. Therefore, martial artists had to incorporate dramatic moves to win applause. With the passage of time, their disciples or mimickers would popularize these showy moves. These people might be truly skilled in kung fu and perform these showy moves only for a living. Anyway, these moves would be useless in real combat. Though showy kung fu would not endure the test of time, it would impede the popularization of real kung fu and mislead public opinion. Throughout history, some elaborate real kung fu had become extinct, while many forms of showy kung fu came into being.

In the Republican era, when martial art was officially

valued and commonly admired, it was common to practice kung fu. This era also witnessed radical changes in the Chinese mindset. These changes influenced the Chinese population in all aspects and of course exerted a profound influence on martial arts. Inspired by Einstein's theory of relativity, Zhang Junmai, a former member of the Imperial Academy, who had studied in Japan and Germany made a speech in 1923. He said that science could not address the problems of life and warned that it was problematic to overemphasize the functions of science. At that time, many intellectuals believed that these theories would hold back scientific promotion and development in China. Back then, China was marked by backwardness in scientific development, and most of the population wanted to find a solution to solve the country's problems through science. The scientific intellectuals emphasized on the necessity of adopting the Western science without questioning the theory of "omnipotence of science." Therefore, this awakening process to seek scientific solutions did not end in diversified and inclusive thoughts but dogmatic conclusions that took no critical view of science. Since then, as an extension of scientism, the idea to see man as a mechanism made of matter caused serious dissociation and imbalance between the spiritual and material domains of the Chinese. It is evident that we used to neglect the significance of traditional moral values on ethnic mindset. With the thriving of materialism, the Chinese population seldom cares about the transition from martial arts to Taoist thinking. The descendants of renowned martial artists refused to practice kung fu, and disciples who would like to spend time practicing decreased in number in a radical manner.

Generally speaking, truly scientific attitudes are supposed to be inclusive in the first place, and science should explore the essence of everything on the basis of phenomena. The public had long confused "technology" with "science," breeding scientism and a biased sense of science that maintains that everything that cannot be testified by modern science is superstition. This assumption has neglected the existence of "phenomenon." Misled by this false assumption, people tend to materialize body and quantify martial arts. *Qigong* and martial skills that are effective in subduing a stronger opponent are believed to be unscientific and impossible.

The Western modern logic is built on two categories of "truth": One is extensional truth, which can be quantified and verified; the other is intensional truth, which is subjectively affirmed but denied in logic practice. The Chinese philosophy holds that truth is reality, while reality is truth, which differs from the former two categories and should be defined as intuitional truth. The so-called "intuitional truth" is about experiencing what's true about this world on the premise of confirming the meaning of the world itself, rather than overlooking its meaning by observing the world from a subjective perspective. For kung fu practitioners, transcending beyond their own limitations and achieving the oneness between heaven and man is possible in such philosophical context. However, in the common Chinese mindset, there is a tendency to neglect intuitional truth as celebrated in traditional Chinese culture and ignore the time-honored wisdom due to obsession with so-called science and an absolutist understanding of "truth," catalyzing hostility to metaphysics. In this context, believers in traditional martial arts gradually declined in number, as the birth, development, and practice of traditional martial arts are closely related to metaphysics.

Internal strife and dynastic changes led to the

1 2
3 4

1–4 Artworks by Martin Klimas, a German artist; we can feel the explosive power of kung fu at a critical moment. The artist has fully captured the hidden dignity and beauty of kung fu.

extinction of many boxing varieties. Ruling class bans on martial arts erected great obstacles for the popularization and inheritance of martial arts. Technical revolutions on the battlefield led to the withdrawal of cavalry. Therefore, the impressive riding and combat skills of the Chinese cavalry went extinct. The transformation of the public mindset triggered doubts over martial art theories and relevant historical documents. The modern concept of martial arts has unfortunately weakened time-honored combat skills. Political campaigns destroyed the community of martial artists. Today, the only child in the family would mostly hold back from martial training out of fear of hardships. It is a common saying that only the best will survive the test of time. However, sometimes it happens the other way around. Only the mediocre remains while the essence is lost with the passage of time, which is the case with Chinese martial arts. This phenomenon deserves serious consideration. In the 1930s, more than 2,000 varieties of traditional boxing were documented. By the 1980s, only 280 of the 2,000 had survived, while only 28 of them had authentic inheritors.

The landscape remains unchanged after millennia. Martial artists are still committed to the promotion and popularization of kung fu.

合为贵

HARMONY AND INCLUSIVENESS OF CHINESE KUNG FU

We cannot identify meridians or acupuncture points through dissection. Do they really exist? In recent years, scientists have utilized infrared thermography and liquid crystal thermography, ultrasonic photography, and other technologies to prove the existence of meridians or acupuncture points. Simply put, meridians act like channels to transport energy, while acupuncture points are pivots on the route. With these research findings, many countries have established comprehensive appraisal systems for traditional Chinese medicine, and acupuncture and Chinese herbal medicine have started to be globally accepted. Foreigners marvel at the fact that the Chinese ancestors could grasp such a complicated science millennia ago. Having incorporated medical knowledge, martial artists of various schools had invented distinctive

圖 經 內

Chart of the Inner Warp portrays human organs and meridians. It is closely associated with longevity, health maintenance and nature cultivation in traditional Chinese medicine.

skills such as attacking the acupuncture points or punching them, which is intended to disturb the internal energy circulation and transportation in the bodies of their opponents or cause local spasm by paralyzing the nerves. My mother used to live with her grandfather in Guangdong in her childhood. Her grandfather practiced martial arts every day and was skilled in barehanded fighting and cudgel play. She had seen how he had subdued an armed gang leader by attacking his acupuncture points and later persuading him to behave himself by restoring his inner circulation. He had utilized his own kung fu skills to prevent a fight irrelevant to his own interests. He was gentle in attack and smiled during persuasion, which exemplified the expectations of a traditional Chinese martial artist who has been influenced by the doctrine of the mean, a Confucian tenet. No one made a fuss over this incident, which implied that other martial artists were also capable of attacking the acupuncture points.

Chinese martial arts, being a common cultural heritage, should not be restricted by national boundaries. Existing boxing varieties are mostly accessible to foreign practitioners. For example, Wing Chun is commonly accepted for its pragmatism and has become an integral part of the combat training in USMC, U.S. Navy Seals, FBI, SEK in Germany, KAID in France, NDCS in Italy, and Special Forces Group in Belgium. I have met with some outstanding European Wing Chun practitioners who have grasped the essence of this boxing variety. Of course, some foreign practitioners just have beautiful moves. I once saw a champion in a cudgel play contest in a European country. He made fabulous poses and shouted in a deterring way. His muscular build also added to the aesthetic value of his performance. However, when rivaling with

functions, and how to further explore physical potentials." According to him, *qigong* and exceptional functions, just like theories on traditional Chinese medicine, should be studied within an advanced scientific framework. Under his guidance, staff in Beijing Aerospace Medical Engineering Research Institute started to research somatic functions in 1984. On the basis of phenomena, the researchers have profoundly explored the exceptional somatic functions from ESP (extrasensory perception) and PK (psychokinesis) perspectives with an objective and scientific attitude. The marriage between intuitional truth and extensional truth provides a brand-new perspective for traditional Chinese martial arts.

A genius is always one step ahead of existing knowledge and technology. Scientists such as Einstein have brought up the notion of multiple-dimensional space, which is reminiscent of extra-space celebrated in both Buddhist and Taoist thoughts. For example, it is believed that an accomplished practitioner can gain transcendence by "jumping out of the three dimensions and staying out of the five elements." In the last century, the theory of relativity has proven that there is a relative relationship between mass and energy, activity and inertia, tininess and greatness, and time and space. The well-known equation of $E = mc^2$ leads to the conclusion that the mass is unreleased energy while energy is released mass. This conclusion reminds us of the Buddhist belief that holds that "all reality is a phantom, and all phantoms are real." Free alternations between mass and energy, if applied to the human body in the future, will produce many unknown domains. Considering this, why should we deny our dreams to travel in the air and glide on water?

Genetic technology is most closely involved with somatic research. We have to take a critical view of this

others, his cudgel fell to the ground several times, which indicated that he had not acquired the combat skills. In order to understand the essence of the Chinese martial arts, a practitioner has to immerse himself in a larger context in the first place. Many Western practitioners start by reading Taoist literature and incorporating its philosophical principles into life, aiming to achieve a consistency between their knowledge and behavior. This consistency is significant to the understanding of Chinese martial arts.

As time goes by, the time-honored metaphysical experience had finally joined hands with scientific experiments. Qian Xuesen was one of the founders and pioneers of somatic science. Known as China's "Father of Space Technology," "Father of the Missile," and "Father of the Automatic Control," Qian defined somatic science as a subject to study "body functions, how to preserve body science, as it is a double-edged sword. We can foresee the inexhaustible positive and negative possibilities, and the creation of Spider-Man and his enemies proves people's awareness of this point. Findings in quantum physics facilitate an understanding of the subtle microworld, thus initiating research on "quantum body." Do not make a quick judgment by interpreting the body as a complex collection of cells, tissue, and organs, as it is also plausible to see it as a tranquil, flowing, tangible, and conscious living intelligence from the quantum perspective. In this sense, it is possible to make changes and adjustments to the body by controlling subjectivities, which is consistent

with the ultimate goal for Taoist practitioners.

While talking about martial arts in the future, we might think of the combat skills of Optimus Prime in *The Matrix* (1999), Neo's Shaolin cudgel play that enables him to confront hundreds of enemies, or the jedi's miraculous lightsabers or their mysterious Force in *Star Wars* (1977). Movie directors and martial artists have made joint efforts to create films that represent a romantic illusion integrating future science and ancient kung fu. As to the future of kung fu, I just want to say, "May the Force be with you."

1
2

1 With this installation, artist Luo Si employs sculpture and modern optics to present human body's unknown possibilities. The artist referred to Michelangelo Buonarroti's *The Creation of Adam* for the man's posture.

2 *1.2 Meters* by Chinese artist Liu Jianhua provides a new perspective. The artist constructs scenes which integrate both traditional aesthetics and futurism with ordinary iron wires.

AFTERWORD

In 2002, I was walking with a friend from North America in a lane in South China, when he pointed at a passerby and asked me whether he knew kung fu. I was surprised by his question, but he replied, "In the movies, slim Chinese are all kung fu practitioners. Are they also fake, just like Santa Clause?"

In 2004, I was traveling through Vietnamese towns on a long-distance bus. Most of the passengers were Westerners. The bus broke down on the way, and for a while we were stuck in the wilderness. Before our eyes were shabby residences and several restaurants with problematic sanitary conditions. A topless one-legged man was dining in a restaurant, indifferent to flies buzzing around his bowls. I was walking around when I found that some fellow passengers were following behind me, though keeping a certain distance. That scene reminded me of America's Western movies and also China's swordsmen movies. I had no idea how this absurd sense of sternness and desolation came into being. When I crossed the road, they followed. I had some noodles in a drugstore, while they followed suit. When the bus hit the road again, all the passengers were relieved. The original seating order was disrupted. A European young man sat next to me timidly and whispered to me, "You know kung fu, don't you?" I asked him why. He answered, "You are Chinese. Of course you know kung fu. Everyone on the bus thinks that you are a kung fu practitioner." On hearing his words, I suddenly realized that they had projected their fantasy about kung fu on me, which had engendered a sense of security in the wilderness.

I'm actually an artist. Whenever I participate in art exhibitions, artists from other countries ask me about kung fu. Therefore, I started to think about writing a book on kung fu.

Wushu, in the Chinese vocabulary, is an umbrella term for combat techniques of various schools. Kung fu is a profound notion referring to moral edification obtained through long-standing *wushu* training. Currently, this notion has extended beyond *wushu*. Anyone who has acquired a certain technique through self-training can be called a practitioner of kung fu.

The most enticing aspect of Chinese kung fu involves "the weak overcoming the strong," which is associated with China's ancient history. Nomadic tribes beyond the Great Wall were blessed with fine horses, meat-based diets, and strong bodies, while the agricultural peoples on the other side of the Great Wall prided themselves on their glorious civilization, strategies, and wisdom. Whenever there was a military conflict, soldiers from the farming civilization were always concerned with how to utilize their infantry to defeat the stronger cavalry. This mentality gradually laid a psychological foundation for the Chinese martial arts. In addition, Taoist thoughts also inspired the development of Chinese *wushu*. Just as the great Chinese philosopher Laozi maintained, the weak can overcome the strong, while the yielding can conquer the unyielding.

I did have some access to kung fu and thus knew some accomplished practitioners in the real sense. It was from them that I came to know various schools of kung fu and their histories, which I shared with the readers here so that even friends on the other side of the ocean can have an understanding of the history and the current situation of Chinese kung fu and the life of accomplished practitioners.

Western audiences fell in love with kung fu because of the kung fu movies they watched, and it was the same with Eastern youngsters. In a darkened theater, the swordsmen who were battling on the screen created kung fu dreams for us. For years, I have been a devoted fan of kung fu movies. In this book, I wanted to share my feelings about kung fu with readers via words and images. I also hoped to shed light on and inspire thoughts over the future development of kung fu through philosophical thinking and scientific hypotheses.

Chinese *wushu* thoughts are mostly based on *The Book of Changes*. This book maintains that the *Qian* diagrams consist of the essence of "original," "penetrating," "advantageous," and "correct and firm," known as *yuan*, *heng*, *li*, and *zhen* in Chinese, which represent the four stages of kung fu practice respectively. *Yuan* stands for the beginning, *heng* for familiarity with movements, *li* for a profound understanding of force, and *zhen* for divinity. I hope this book has helped establish a bond between you and Chinese kung fu, bring you *yuan* in kung fu, and inspire a new route in your search for life values, through which you will head for divinity.

THE ART OF CHINESE KUNG FU

Editor in Chief: Guo Guang

Project Editors: Mang Yu, Ricoe Jen

English Editor: Jenny Qiu

Translator: Coral Yee

Book Designer: Peng Tao

Author: Zhang Zheyi

Visual Effects Coordinator: Lili Chen

Project Coordinator: Meng Zhigang

Photographers: Liu Xianbiao, Meng Zhigang, Ding Sukai, Wen Bin, Liu Ende, Li Bing, Li Shun, Shi Guowei, Liu Bin, Guo Jian, Guo Guozhu, Neng Ying, Lili Chen, Zhang Li, Wang Zhipeng, Caius Nesvadba (UK)

Special Thanks:

Images of ink and wash paintings on pages 8-9, 62-63 and 144-145 are provided by artist Xiao Shunzhi.

Images of installation art *Alien Bamboo* on pages 10, 26, 42, 52, 66, 114, 146 and 152 are provided by artist Xi Hua.

Image of artworks on page 148 by Martin Klimas is provided by Other Gallery.

Image of installation art on page 154 is provided by artist Luo Si.

Image of artwork on page 155 by Liu Jianhua is provided by Pace Beijing.

First published in the United States of America in 2014

Gingko Press, Inc
1321 Fifth Street
Berkeley, CA 94710, USA
Phone(510)8981195
Fax(510)8981196
email: books@gingkopress.com
www.gingkopress.com

ISBN: 978-1-58423-569-9

Printed in China